Mike Rose, May 14, 1944 – August 15, 2021.
Photograph courtesy of UCLA School of
Education & Information Studies.

Writing Program Administration

Journal of the
Council of Writing Program Administrators

Guest Editors

Angela Clark-Oates .... California State University, Sacramento
Aurora M. Matzke .... Azusa Pacific University
Sherry Rankins-Robertson .... University of Central Florida

Editorial Board

Nancy Bou Ayash .... University of Washington
David Blakesley .... Clemson University
Beth Brunk-Chavez .... University of Texas at El Paso
Sheila Carter-Tod .... University of Denver
Chen Chen .... Winthrop University
Sherri Craig .... West Chester University
Casie Fedukovich .... North Carolina State University
Carolyn (Collie) Fulford .... North Carolina Central University
David Green .... Howard University
Teresa Grettano .... University of Scranton
Sarah Z. Johnson .... Madison College
Alexandria Lockett .... Spelman College
Staci Perryman-Clark .... Western Michigan University
Patti Poblete... Henderson State University
Amy Ferdinandt Stolley .... Grand Valley State University
Darci Thoune.. University of Wisconsin–LaCrosse
Peter Vandenberg .... DePaul University

Production and distribution of *WPA: Writing Program Administration* is managed by Parlor Press.

Council of Writing Program Administrators

Executive Board

Susan Thomas, President... University of Sydney
Lilian Mina, Vice President .... University of Alabama at Birmingham
Mark Blaauw-Hara, Past President .... University of Toronto Mississauga
Patti Poblete... Henderson State University
Melvin Beavers... University of Arkansas at Little Rock
Al Harahap .... University of Oklahoma
Erin Lehman.. Ivy Tech Community College of Indiana
Annie Del Principe ....Kingsborough Community College
Derek Mueller..Virginia Tech
Katherine Daily O'Meara ....St. Norbert College
Sarah Snyder .... Arizona Western College
Julia Voss .... Santa Clara University

Ex Officio Members

Mary McCall, Treasurer .... North Dakota State University
Kelley Blewett, Secretary .... Indana University East
Shirley K Rose, Co-Director CES................................... Arizona State University
Michael Pemberton, Co-Director, CES .... Georgia Southern University

Guide for Authors

WPA: Writing Program Administration publishes empirical and theoretical research on issues in writing program administration. We publish a wide range of research in various formats, research that not only helps both titled and untitled administrators of writing programs do their jobs, but also helps our discipline advance academically, institutionally, and nationally.
Possible topics of interest include:

- writing faculty professional development
- writing program creation and design
- uses for national learning outcomes and statements that impact writing programs
- classroom research studies
- labor conditions: material, practical, fiscal
- WAC/WID/WC/CAC (or other sites of communication/writing in academic settings)
- writing centers and writing center studies
- teaching writing with electronic texts (multimodality) and teaching in digital spaces
- theory, practice, and philosophy of writing program administration
- outreach and advocacy
- curriculum development
- writing program assessment
- WPA history and historical work
- national and regional trends in education and their impact on WPA work
- issues of professional advancement and writing program administration
- diversity and WPA work
- writing programs in a variety of educational locations (SLACs, HBCUs, two-year colleges, Hispanic schools, non-traditional schools, dual credit or concurrent enrollment programs, prison writing programs)
- interdisciplinary work that informs WPA practices

This list is meant to be suggestive, not exhaustive. Contributions must be appropriate to the interests and concerns of the journal and its readership. The editors welcome empirical research (quantitative as well as qualitative), historical research, and theoretical, essayistic, and practical pieces.

Submission Guidelines

Please check the *WPA* website for complete submissions guidelines and to download the required coversheet. In general, submissions should:

- be a maximum 7,500 words;
- be styled according to either the *MLA Handbook* (9th edition) or the *Publication Manual of the American Psychological Association* (7th edition), as appropriate to the nature of your research;

- include an abstract (maximum 200 words);
- contain no identifying information;
- be submitted as a .doc or .docx format file; and
- use tables, notes, figures, and appendices sparingly and judiciously.

Submissions that do not follow these guidelines or that are missing the cover page will be returned to authors before review.

Reviews

WPA:Writing Program Administration publishes both review essays of multiple books and reviews of individual books related to writing programs and their administration. If you are interested in reviewing texts or recommending books for possible review, please contact the book review editor at wpabookreviews@gmail.com.

Announcements and Calls

Relevant announcements and calls for papers may be published as space permits. Announcements should not exceed 500 words, and calls for proposals or participation should not exceed 1,000 words. Submission deadlines in calls should be no sooner than January 1 for the fall issue and June 1 for the spring issue. Please email your calls and announcements to wpaeditors@gmail.com and include the text in both the body of the message and as a .doc or .docx attachment.

Correspondence

Correspondence relating to the journal, submissions, or editorial issues should be sent to wpaeditors@gmail.com.

Subscriptions

WPA: Writing Program Administration is published twice per year—fall and spring—by the Council of Writing Program Administrators. Members of the council receive a subscription to the journal and access to the *WPA* archives as part of their membership. Join the council at http://wpacouncil.org. Information about library subscriptions is available at http://wpacouncil.org/aws/CWPA/pt/sp/journal-subscriptions.

Writing Program Administration

Journal of the
Council of Writing Program Administrators
Volume 45.2 (Spring 2022)

Mike Rose: Teacher and Scholar, Writer and Friend

Editors' Introduction 12
    Angela Clark-Oates, Aurora Matzke, and
    Sherry Rankins-Robertson

Introduction: Remembering Mike Rose 17
    David Bartholomae

"Remembering Mike Rose" recalls 40+ years of friendship and collaboration.

Interlude I: Mike Rose in This Hallway 23
    John Paul Tassoni

Mike Rose valued working-class, first-generation students' ways of knowing and life on the boundaries of academia's center stages. This narrative essay illustrates the temporal and spatial trajectories of such values, the ways that Rose's faith in them informs/is informed by students of writing, their teachers, and writing program administrators.

Section I: "Remedial" Education (Basic Writing)

Mike Rose: Remediating Academia via Inclusive Pedagogy 26
    Kristy Liles Crawley

Celebrating Mike Rose's contributions to the field of Composition and Rhetoric, this tribute recognizes Rose's examination of the harmful "remedial" label in writing studies, honors his call for prioritizing inclusive pedagogy over correctness, and demonstrates that his call for inclusion maintains its relevance today through PARS, an inclusive pedagogical approach.

Reminding Us Why We Are Here: Mike Rose's Legacy for Basic Writing 30
Lynn Reid

In this essay, the author explores why, over a career that spanned more than four decades, Mike Rose frequently critiqued existing conceptions of remediation. Rather than calling for its elimination, the author argues, Rose challenged teacher-scholars to reimagine our work to provide support for students whose academic experiences prior to college did not put them on equal footing with their peers.

Once You're Seen You Can't Unsee 33
Christina Saidy

This contribution describes the way that Mike Rose weaved story, research, and commentary, and challenged us to question simple counting as a way to understand readiness, competence, and literacy and to see student writers deeply. Rose's work continues to have deep implications for the work of WPAs and writing teacher/scholars.

Interlude II: Lives in the Complexity..36
Douglas Hesse

Mike Rose's early teaching and writing administration, reflected in conversations and documents from the late 1970's to early 1990s, use pragmatic cognitivist frameworks to further progressive goals. While he modified and recontextualized this framework as he became an elder statesman and public intellectual, he maintained these views. The author asserts, from Rose's life and career, contemporary WPAs might take three lessons: Write regularly, including for personal interests, not only disciplinary fealty; Value identities as teachers and writers as equal to administrative advancement; Practice passions kindly.

Section II: Classism and Racism

Encountering Lives on the Boundary: Mike Rose as Methodologist for Centering Minoritized Writers 44
Ray Rosas

This essay considers how Mike Rose's work might be taken up to advance antiracist writing program administration. Throughout his career, Rose centered the experiences of minoritized writers through a variety of naturalistic methods. The author contends that Rose's equity-driven, emic-oriented research contributions provide a generative resource for emerging antiracist work.

Whatever Happened to Average? Heeding Mike Rose's Call 48
Kelly Ritter

This brief essay puts Mike Rose's Lives on the Boundary in conversation with recent scholarship on socioeconomic disparities present in pre-college credit programs in high schools (specifically Advanced Placement), and the effects these disparities later have on first-year college students who are also first-generation.

"Becoming fully and richly literate": Teaching Antiracism to Bring More Lives from the Boundaries 52
Kathleen Turner Ledgerwood

This article examines Mike Rose's work in Lives on the Boundary *as a foundational exploration of classist practices in writing. Rose calls for a rich literacy is a precursor to today's calls to expand literacy. A critical language approach helps pave a path for composition to incorporate antiracist practices*

Mike Rose, the Rust Belt, and Me 56
Marjorie Stewart

A chance meeting with Mike Rose gave the author of this essay a chance to revisit his work. This serendipitous encounter focused on the love of story, on a mutual passion for helping underprepared students, and shared rust belt backgrounds.

The Reading Labs: Pedagogical History and Humane Design 59
Luis E. Poza and Manuel Luis Espinoza

This brief essay describes Reading Labs, a pedagogical intervention implemented to support novice social science students with reading complex primary legal documents and composing analytic summaries and other collegiate writing. In this overview, the authors highlight the social nature of learning: how meanings were negotiated among participants deciphering laws and court opinions, how questions and peer feedback helped sharpen arguments and voice in students' written work. In so doing, the authors evoke Mike Rose's own work in writing programs across levels, relying on small, intimate groupings of students, serious regard given to their intellectual efforts including errors, and a pedagogy marked by encouragement and gentle questioning.

Interlude III: "Just as I have a mind": Mike Rose and the
Intelligence of Ordinary People 63
    John Trimbur

    This essay looks at the social democratic roots of Mike Rose's belief in the intelligence of ordinary people and the educability of poor and working-class kids currently bypassed by the education system. His later work, especially The Mind at Work, *challenges the narrowing effects of the division of mental and manual labor in class society, imagining instead the inventive interplay of mind, heart, and hand.*

Section III: Challenges in Education

Mike Rose's Two-Year College Advocacy 68
    Darin L. Jensen and Cheryl Hogue Smith

    As community college faculty, the authors know that Mike Rose was a champion of our institutions. The dialogue here reflects both his personal influence on the authors as literacy workers and on two-year college English studies.

"I Didn't Know How Else to Get It Right":
Lives on the Boundary as an Invitation to Public Intellectualism 72
    Ryan Skinnell

    For nearly four decades, Mike Rose was one of the most successful public intellectuals in rhetoric and composition, and he routinely encouraged his colleagues to engage more intentionally with non-academic audiences. Lives on the Boundary *continues to provide a valuable model for considering how and why.*

My Mike Rose: The Library, Mom, and Critical Reading in
Lives on the Boundary 76
    Alice S. Horning

    This piece captures the author's personal experience with Mike Rose that occurred as a by-product of her finding, more or less by chance, and reading Lives on the Boundary, *a book that captures important features of academic critical literacy of students then and now. To honor his legacy, writing studies faculty and all others in higher education must work to develop students' ability to read, write, speak and listen effectively, efficiently and critically.*

Stepping Back to Step Forward: A Tribute to Mike Rose 81
Anthony Lince

The following article provides a narrative which details how Mike Rose positively influenced the author's teaching practices, specifically as it relates to assessment and grading.

A Different Kind of Hunger 85
Thomas Newkirk

Mike Rose's Lives on the Boundary *came out a few years after Richard Rodriguez's elegiac memoir* Hunger of Memory *and can be viewed as a powerful response. While Rose is sharply critical of the failure of modern universities to teach the under-prepared, he demonstrated, through his own story, that this instruction can happen if there is a more personal and intimate attempt to demystify academic work.*

Interlude IV: Mike Rose: Helping All of Us Do Better 88
Kathleen Blake Yancey

Mike Rose left us with many legacies, three of which I highlight here: his re-conceptualization of school as part of the public; his reflection on both the human act of teaching and the promise of teaching more humanely; and the need for teachers to share widely what we have learned from our teaching.

Section IV: Human and Inclusive Approaches to Education

Keeping the Faith: Rediscovering the Hope of Mike Rose 94
Julie Lindquist

This essay argues that Mike Rose's work created a distinctive pathway for writing program administration. Rose understood education as a deeply human project—one steeped in questions of equity and educational principles. A return to Rose's work simultaneously demonstrates the persistence of questions regarding what counts as education as well as how inclusion and exclusion are fostered by our attempts to define "higher" education.

Listening to Mike Rose: Education Is a Grand Human Enterprise 100
Shane A. Wood

Mike Rose dedicated his life to teaching and writing about education. He influenced teachers and students across the nation, and the author was fortunate to get to know him over the last two years. What stood out in their conversations were Rose's curiosity and commitment to exploring human nature.

Mike Rose: Insights from the Classroom 105
Mike Palmquist

While many of the articles in this special issue focus on contributions Mike Rose made through his scholarly work, this essay provides a discussion of his work in the classroom. Drawing on a graduate seminar taught in Fall 1986, when Rose was serving as a visiting professor at Carnegie Mellon University, the article explores key aspects of Rose's approach to designing and teaching a course.

Notes on Mike Rose 112
Lisa Moore

A farewell to Mike Rose on his unexpected death, this personal remembrance recounts Rose's generous guidance on the discipline for a new Comp/Rhet editor and his very human capacity for empathy and insight expressed by his devotion to the value of every person whatever their circumstances and the craft of writing.

Mike Rose and the University of the People 115
Shirin Vossoughi and Manuel Espinoza

This reprinted blog offers a dialogue framed as "a siblings' tribute to a giant" between Rose's students.

The Small Stuff 118
John Alberti

Drawing on the author's experience as a graduate student in Mike Rose's practicum on teaching, the essay discusses the foundational importance of "small things," as Rose called them. The author describes how Rose's teaching provided him an opportunity to experience the "micro-evidence of care" in Rose's classroom interactions and the profound effect such a "small thing" had on the author's formation as a teacher and scholar.

Conclusion: In Memory of Mike Rose 123
Ellen Cushman

This essay recognizes the enduring impact of Mike Rose on the field of writing and literacy studies, the quality of his mind, and his dedication to education, teaching, and learning.

Selected Works of Mike Rose 131
Kobena Bannerman-Jones

Editors' Introduction

Angela Clark-Oates, Aurora Matzke, and
 Sherry Rankins-Robertson

Mike Rose: Teacher and Scholar, Writer and Friend

As a scholar with more than four decades of contributions to the field, Mike Rose set the stage for how the field of composition and rhetoric would grapple with basic writing, working-class rhetorics, and open-access education. Although it is impossible to quantify his impact, his broad reach is certainly evidenced by the twelve books he authored and edited, over sixty articles in print, numerous book chapters, and his uncountable speaking engagements and public works. Beyond the scholarship that Mike contributed to the field, he leaves a legacy that is evidenced with the scholars who have been shaped by his works. Throughout his life, Rose wrote prolifically on public education policies and reform, often troubling the easy answers academics give themselves regarding how to foster intrinsically motivated learning.

From *Lives on the Boundary* to *The Mind at Work* to *Back to School*, Rose's work focuses extensively on socioeconomics and the impacts, challenges, and opportunities present in higher education for the working class in the United States. Rose brought attention to adult learners and reminded us all that class-based decisions regarding readiness to learn are nothing but a lack of imagination on the part of those in positions of power. In the introduction to *The Mind at Work*, Rose argues, "Measures of intellectual ability and assumptions about it are woven throughout [my] history. So I've been thinking about this business of intelligence for a long time: the way we decide who's smart and who isn't, the way the work someone does feeds into that judgment, and the effect such judgment has on our sense of who we are and what we can do" (xiii). The questions of who we are and what we can do rest at the focal point of much, if not all of, the scholarship in writing program administration. And it is with this knowledge, and respect for Mike Rose's leadership and contributions, that we have compiled this special issue.

Throughout his career in teaching, writing, and research, Rose exposed the dualistic thinking so pervasive in our public, legislative, and academic settings by using the lived experiences of the working class, students, and teachers to challenge "the single story" of learning. In her podcast *On Being*, Kristen Tippet reminds us that Mike Rose's "expansive wisdom" makes it possible to disrupt our tendency to view learning too narrowly, encouraging us to illuminate the blending, the hybridity of the process, the coalescence of the physical, human, and cognitive.

Working from this challenge, contributors in this special issue share how Mike Rose has influenced their "civic imagination on big subjects at the heart of who we are—schooling, social class, and the deepest meaning of vocation" (Tippet). The texts presented within the issue show how Rose's work has not only profoundly impacted our past, but also continues to inform our vision for the future of writing program administration. In particular, submissions were sought from those who identify as working class, first gen, from historically, minoritized backgrounds, and those who worked with Rose and/or his contributions to the field. We hope that the special issue serves to trouble easy answers about Rose's work, as we honor his lasting contributions. In this vein, contributors work to answer the following questions:

- What challenges Rose's work in light of new developments and perspectives within the field?
- How might Rose's work be blended with emerging ideas across generational and/or institutional lines?
- How does it demonstrate an understanding of the difficulties writers face based on class, race, economics, region?
- How might we celebrate the impact of Rose's work in the areas of access, accessibility, community partnership, socio-economic equity/justice/assistance, and/or other of Rose's foci?

By centering narratives, dialogues, observations, and conversations, Rose illuminated multiple and diverse perspectives and experiences about teaching, learning, and working. To understand how his work compels us to imagine the future of writing program administration, we also present collaborative and polyvocal works that illustrate textured and nuanced understanding of the constraints and tensions that emerge in educational research and education policy about what counts as learning and whose learning counts. In the words of Mike Rose, "it is hope that drives the writing, hope that careful analysis and the right phrasing might in some small, small way open a space to think anew" (*An Open Language*, Introduction).

To facilitate this work, the special issue opens with an introduction written by David Bartholomae, who takes readers through some of Rose's first works, as well as some of his last. Readers move through four sections, which bring together conversations around "remedial" education; classism and racism in education; challenges in education; and human and inclusive approaches to education. The introduction and four sections are set apart with interludes. These interludes work to introduce and connect concepts throughout the issue, as well as serve as moments of historicity within the field–placing Rose's work in the larger context of the field and beyond. Ellen Cushman's text closes the collection with a close look at the professional and personal persona that Rose championed throughout his career.

This issue serves as not only a stirring tribute to the work of Mike Rose, but also as a reminder of how much work is yet to be done to truly construct educational spaces that allow for all and any to imagine who they want to be and what they want to do. As you sit down with this text, you may want to return to Shane Wood's opening episode of *Pedagogue* (located at https://www.pedagoguepodcast.com) to hear Mike Rose reflect on his experiences as a writing teacher. Rose reminds us of the privilege and importance of our work in the classroom; he says "there's not many occupations that provide that opportunity to get close into people's lives and help them grow in a way they want to grow" (Wood). You may find some delight in traveling along Rose's narrative of self discovery in his writing about his family history, with childhood and family images included, in one of Rose's final publications, "Searching for Tommy and Rosie." He writes, "It is through the telling of her stories that I'm finding a way to live the rest of my life—stories of work and opportunity and the barriers to it, of finding meaning in the hand we're dealt, of her dreams for me, of desire that propels us forward or flattens us with a broken heart" (Rose). Perhaps you will find yourself, near this one-year anniversary of Mike Rose's passing, rereading Kevin Dettmar's celebration of Rose's rippling influence on education in "The Teacher Who Changed How We Teach Writing." Dettmar writes, "His work heralded a paradigm shift in the way that writing is taught in our educational system, from elementary school through college." We invite you to savor the issue, as we all strive to "think anew" on how Rose's work served to shape the past, present, and future of writing program administration.

Acknowledgments

In the spirit of Mike Rose's generous heart, we would be remiss if we did not acknowledge several people for their work on this collection. We thank the twenty-five authors who shared their encounters with Mike and the influence of his works on their teaching and scholarship. We also want to thank Kobena Bannerman-Jones, who worked diligently on the extensive bibliography. Kobe's contribution showcases Rose's contribution not only as a scholar in our field but also as a public intellectual. As Duane Roen reminds us in his 2014 CWPA plenary address: "Mike Rose, who seems to move effortlessly between the academy and the public sphere, . . . uses a prose style that is accessible and elegant . . . mak[ing] even the most complex ideas understandable. In his books, as in his life, he melds the academic, the professional, the civic, and the personal arenas of life." We are grateful to the past presidents of CWPA who offered support to this editorial team, particularly for the kind and thorough feedback of Doug Hesse and the editorial eye of Duane Roen. This journal would not be possible without the work of David Blakesley and Parlor Press. We appreciate the CWPA executive board, who supported a special issue on our colleague Mike Rose, who lived the roles of teacher and scholar, writer, and friend.

Works Cited

Dettmar, Kevin. "The Teacher Who Changed How We Teach Writing." *The New Yorker*, 14 Oct. 2021, https://www.newyorker.com/culture/postscript/the-teacher-who-changed-how-we-teach-writing

Roen, Duane. "Writing Program Faculty and Administrators as Public Intellectuals: Opportunities and Challenges." Plenary Speech. Annual meeting of the Council of Writing Program Administrators, 19 July 2014, Normal, IL.

Rose, Mike. "Searching for Tommy and Rosie." *The American Scholar*, 3 Mar. 2022, https://theamericanscholar.org/searching-for-tommy-and-rosie/

Wood, Shane. "Episode 1: Mike Rose (pt. 1)." *Pedagogue*, 9 May 2021, https://www.pedagoguepodcast.com/episodes.html

Angela Clark-Oates (she/her/hers) is associate professor of composition and rhetoric in the English department at California State University, Sacramento. She recently finished a six-year term as the writing program administrator and will begin a new administrative role as the graduation writing assessment coordinator. Her research interests include writing program administration and faculty learning, feminist rhetorics and pedagogies, literacy studies, and assessment. Her scholarship has been published in *The Journal of Writing Assessment* and *Communication Design Quarterly*. She has also published in the anthologies *Stories from First-Year Composition: Pedagogies that Foster Student Agency and Writing Identity*, *Women's Way of Making*, *The Framework for Success in Postsecondary Writing: Scholarship and Applications*, *A Fresh Approach to the Common Core State Standards in Research and Writing*, and *Working with Faculty Writers*.

Aurora Matzke (she/her/hers) is a professor of writing and director of tutoring, writing, and speaking centers in Southern California. Her recent work includes publications and presentations on systems theories, mentorship, and feminist coalition building. Her research, teaching, and administrative work focus on open access education, educational support systems, and k-16 transitions.

Sherry Rankins-Robertson (she/her/ella) is chair and professor of writing and rhetoric at the University of Central Florida. She has held leadership roles on executive committees and task forces for CWPA, CCCC, and NCTE. Her scholarly interests focus on community-engaged writing, writing program administration, multimodal pedagogies, feminist leadership practices, and faculty well-being. Sherry's passion for student success has fueled her energy to develop successful, sustainable higher education programs to improve students' experiences both on campus and in the community. For the past twenty years, she has taught first-year writing; she also teaches nonfiction writing and graduate-level theory courses. For more than a decade, she has taught writing in prisons. Sherry is a RYT-200 with Yoga Alliance.

Remembering Mike Rose

David Bartholomae

"Remembering Mike Rose" recalls 40+ years of friendship and collaboration.

Mike Rose is gone, and what a loss it is—not only to his many friends and colleagues, but to the profession and to generations of teachers and students whose work was (and will continue to be) informed by his presence. Mike's great contribution to our thinking about teaching and learning was his remarkably deep and generous attention to detail. He wrote from the inside; he wrote about people and places; and he wrote about what mattered. He was tireless and meticulous in his field work. He would engage the "literature" and the issues of the moment, but always as points of reference, not as subjects, and primarily to explain or ground or illuminate the lived moments that made his writing so memorable and so persuasive.

Mike Rose could wander in and out of your life, but when he was there, you knew it and it made a difference. Things slowed down. The conversation sparked. You saw and understood the world differently. He was a master teacher. For me, he was a writer's writer, and I will miss him dearly.

***

I am trying to remember when and where I first met Mike. It must have been the early 80s, before he began working toward the final drafts of *Lives on the Boundary* (published in 1989). I'm sure we must have met at the CCCCs, and I suspect the meeting was brokered by our mutual friend, Joan Feinberg of (then) Bedford Books. After that, there was a group of friends, including Mike and Joan, who began to gather regularly for a long dinner at the annual meeting.

Mike had read my essay, "The Study of Error" (published in 1980) and we had begun a long-distance conversation (mostly letters!) about what was then called "Basic Writing," courses designed for students whose entry into the academy as readers and writers was fraught and difficult, marked by struggle. We didn't even have to warm up to each other. It seemed like we had been having this conversation for years. The talk was easy and animated and loving and fun. We were on the same page. Our professional lives took us this way and that, but we insisted on staying on the same page, even when we weren't.

Around this time, Mike invited me to provide an essay for his edited collection, *When a Writer Can't Write: Studies in Writer's Block and other*

Composing Problems (1985). At this point, I could properly have been called a "cognitivist." ("The Study of Error" used methods drawn from cognitivist work on math and second language learning.) I had just received promotion and tenure, and I had applied for and won a Fulbright Lectureship to teach American literature at the Universidad de Deusto in Bilbao, Spain. I carried notes and books with me on the move to Bilbao, and I had a knapsack filled with 500 student responses to our placement exam. These were to provide the subject matter for my essay, which ended up with the title, "Inventing the University."

The books, on the other hand, were part of a sabbatical project to read my way through the work of Jacques Derrida and Michel Foucault. I hadn't planned to bring them to the essay I was preparing for Mike, but in the end I wrote a very different kind of essay than the one I had proposed for the volume. It began with an epigraph from Foucault's "Discourse on Language":

> Education may well be, as of right, the instrument whereby every individual, in a society like our own, can gain access to any kind of discourse. But we well know that in its distribution, in what it permits and in what it prevents, it follows the well-trodden battlelines of social conflict. Every educational system is a political means of maintaining or of modifying the appropriation of discourse, with the knowledge and the powers it carries with it (227).

Mike was looking for an essay from a cognitivist. I sent him something very different, and he wrote to say, "Whoa. What's up?"

I think my essay came in late; I was out of the country and out of the loop, and what I wrote seemed to have little to do with the core concerns of the volume. I didn't set out to be different, but by the time I wrote the essay I was thinking differently. I can remember the pleasure and the energy I found in the essay once I started to work on it. And so I did what we all do in such a situation; I sent what I had.

I think Mike was initially a little flummoxed. It was a big jump from mental blocks to the prison house of language! I know that we wrote back and forth about the essay. Whatever dissonance I had created, however, couldn't be revised away. It was just a question of whether he wanted the essay in the collection or not. Mike was, as he always was, open and generous and curious and thoughtful. I know that he was interested in what I was doing and saw its importance—and so, in the end, my essay was part of his collection.

Soon after, Mike invited me to read drafts of *Lives on the Boundary*. We wrote back and forth regularly for about a year. Like many writers, the closer Mike got to finishing his book, the more nervous he became. This book was, he knew, his launching point, and he was telling a story that cut close to the bone. Mike was a worrier by nature, and the thought of finishing, of handing his book over to others, became almost paralyzing. He was a charmer, but he was also a gifted and serious writer, and he needed to believe that readers could (and would) not just admire the book but receive his gift, acknowledge the work, understand who he was and what he had accomplished as a writer and a scholar. This was Mike's signature writing block.

He had become stuck while fussing with the Introduction, and he asked me for advice. I suggested moving some paragraphs around, burying his lead a bit, slowing things down, inviting his readers in. It seemed to help. The book of course was an enormous success, and a great achievement, and this all had nothing to do with me. Mike would often remind me, though, that my close reading of his work helped to keep him going at the end, when he was spinning his wheels and losing momentum. This was also typical of Mike—to pass on to others credit that was rightly his own.

***

At the time of his death, we were again in close contact. Each of us was finishing a book. I was beginning to read his new manuscript. He had just finished reading mine. We were both feeling nervous, and we were both looking for one more trusted and sympathetic reader, someone who might acknowledge that what we were doing still mattered. My book, *Like What we Imagine: Writing and the University,* is now in print. At the time of his death, Mike was still working with his agent to find a publisher for his memoir. It had the tentative title, *When the Light Goes On.* Both of our books were, in a sense, a return to beginnings. Mike was writing again about his childhood and his family and about his high school English teacher, Jack McFarland, a key figure in *Lives on the Boundary.* My book is a kind of professional memoir. Two of the chapters speak directly to my last year of teaching at the University of Pittsburgh. An opening chapter is set during my freshman year at Ohio Wesleyan.

I had submitted one of these essays (titled, "Back to Basics") to the *Journal of Basic Writing.* (I had published with *JBW* at the beginning of my career, and I had hoped to publish with them one last time at the end.) The editors sent a copy to Mike for review. Mike sent me a note to let me know that he was reading it. And he added, as he usually did, a detailed critique that went well beyond (and that spoke to me much more frankly than) the letter he had sent to the journal.

He concluded with a note:

> I am finishing up a book, and the conclusion is kicking my ass. (Conclusions for all my books have done so.) I find myself thinking of me and you sitting on the deck of the Crab Shell bar overlooking the Pacific when you told me to reverse the position of the two opening paragraphs in the preface of *Lives on the Boundary*....and friggen' bingo, the thing just popped. Not a praying man, I'm praying for one of those Ah-Ha moments.

I offered to help. He sent me the "Preface" and a link to a brief essay in *The Hedgehog Review,* "The Desk," which I assumed was part of the new book, perhaps part of the conclusion that had stymied him. He said,

> You asked about the Heartbreaking-Work-of-Staggering-Genius that has consumed the last five years of my life. . . . I am going to send you the preface. It'll give you an overview. It begins with a deep dive into the Senior English class that saved my life, but isn't a rehash of *Lives on the Boundary.* I really tried to figure out exactly what the hell happened over that nine months in my late adolescence, and was fortunate to have my teacher explore it with me. . . . from there you'll see what else I did. I hope you like it.

As far as I know, this book is still unpublished, and so I thought it might be appropriate to provide a brief summary, something to keep the book and its possibilities alive and in circulation.

Mike's "Preface" is a straightforward summary of the book's origin and its chapters. The premise for the book is this: Mike goes back to his old neighborhood in South Central Los Angeles, and he sits down again with Jack McFarland, the teacher who changed the course of his life. They reread the books on the old syllabus, they look over Mike's papers, and then they look again, and they talk about teaching and learning, about what they've learned in the classroom and from each other over time.

As a context to this encounter between a student and his teacher, Mike visited schools and talked with other teachers and other students. Over a five-year period, he interviewed one hundred people in all: "They ranged from high schoolers to sixty and seventy year olds, people who grew up in well-to-do neighborhoods and people who grew up in neighborhoods like mine—in a few cases *in* my old neighborhood." And the Preface concludes:

> The deep dive into my life-changing year in Senior English and the similarly transformative experiences of a wide range of other people afford a picture of education at its vibrant best, those times when the mind stirs and schooling is infused with purpose. The composite pic-

ture leads us to think about education in ways that are dramatically different from the mainstream policy narrative about schools that has dominated American culture for a generation. Chapter Eight ("Education for a Meaningful Life") draws from all the book's cases to offer a fresh take on teaching, learning, and motivation, on intelligence and achievement, on the structure of school, and on the goals of education itself. Our bloodless policy talk is reinvigorated with a language of intellectual pleasure, human connection, and the desire for a meaningful life.

"The Desk," on the other hand, is a memory piece with the subtitle: "How the imagination kept the unthinkable at bay." It is a boy's level account of pinched circumstances: a father who is seriously ill, a mother who heads out each day to work as a waitress, an old, empty and somewhat ramshackle house, a lone child. During the day, the boy's imagination turned the ordinary into theaters of fantasy. We shared a number of reference points: our first desk, Sargent Bilko, Buck Rogers, Space Patrol.

I said:

> What a pleasure!—a complicated one, to be sure, but those are the ones that make you say *Wow*. You think you are entering a sentimental account of childhood and childhood's spaces. But then you get: 'As a little boy, there was the soft tunnel under blankets. Once I had the bed to myself, I'd burrow under the quilt imagining passageways to safe mystery.' *Once I had the bed to myself?! As a subordinate clause??!!*
>
> The desk, the cardboard boxes ask to be front and center, but what I couldn't shake was the big bed in front of the front door, and your Dad in it, losing his leg. There is the boy and the boy's world, and he's trying to work it all out. And there is the writer, years later, also trying to work things out. You orchestrate this just brilliantly.

Mike's response was:

> Trying to bring the book I've been working on to market . . . has really been demoralizing, so to get a response like yours to this little piece makes my day and gets some wind back in my sails. You nailed it about the bed. Our house was tiny, so this big, motorized thing humming all day and night consumed everything. Shit, man, my poor father.

And then Mike was gone.

***

Mike was a remarkably productive, visible, and influential scholar. At a time when research was becoming more and more predictable, and when it was addressed to increasingly specialized audiences, Mike Rose provided the striking example of a scholar who could think beyond the expected and who had the ambition to write for the nation.

The evidence for this is in the startling, impressive, and completely unpredictable projects represented on the CV. He has also, however, shown a deep and selfless commitment to the support of teachers, to the support of local and national initiatives affecting the schools, to promoting and refining the uses of writing in American education, and to raising public awareness to the issues that matter in contemporary schooling. He had the ambition to address the broadest audience and he did it with great integrity and great success. Careful, innovative scholarship, attention to local programs and projects, public advocacy on behalf of students, teachers, and workers--this is a rare and distinctive combination, evidence of a person with a generous spirit and with commitments beyond his own career.

Mike helped to shape the public discourse and the public understanding of issues in contemporary education. For years, you could find him on the radio and TV bringing his careful, thoughtful, informed positions to a range of audiences. On several occasions, I heard Mike literally change the tone and pacing of a talk show, a public meeting, or a news broadcast. The room went from noisy to quiet; the talk became thoughtful, careful. It was like magic.

Work Cited

Foucault, Michel. "Discourse of Language" *The Archeology of Knowledge and the Discourse on Language*. Pantheon, 1972.

David Bartholomae is professor of English and the Charles Crow Chair of Expository Writing, Emeritus at the University of Pittsburgh. He has served as the chair of CCCC, the president of the MLA's Associated Departments of English, and as a member of the MLA's Executive Council. His honors include a Chancellor's Distinguished Teaching Award, the ADE/MLA Francis Andrew March Award, the CCC Exemplar Award, the Richard B. Braddock Award (for "The Study of Error") and the Mina Shaughnessy Award (for *Writing on the Margins*). He has published widely on composition and teaching. With Jean Ferguson Carr, he edits the University of Pittsburgh Press book series, *Composition, Literacy, Culture*.

Mike Rose in This Hallway

John Paul Tassoni

Mike Rose valued working-class, first-generation students' ways of knowing and life on the boundaries of academia's center stages. This narrative essay illustrates the temporal and spatial trajectories of such values, the ways that Rose's faith in them informs/is informed by students of writing, their teachers, and writing program administrators.

I stake out the rooms where my conference presentations are scheduled. The arrangement of chairs, their relation to any podium or platform, offers me a sense of how things could play out. Even though spaces reserved for my panels typically look the same, I perform this ritual, conference after conference. These days, I find something reassuring in the room's familiarity. At the same time, I still too often imagine a crowd indifferent to what I've come to say. Picturing myself at the lectern in these moments, I wrestle with some vague feeling of isolation, work to summon instead whatever knowledge and experience I have that brings me here.

Years ago, I was returning from one of these musings when I ran into Mike Rose. Mike was backing himself out of the convention center's grand ballroom. "I came to check out where my talk is," he told me. He stood there in the doorframe, door ajar against his shoulder. Behind his white, curly hair, I could see enough of the theater to anticipate his vast audience. "God," he said, "this room is so big." Although smiling, he looked unnerved. When I read this special issue's call for papers, I right away saw this image: Mike Rose in this hallway linked to countless corridors, channeling hundreds of participants, spilling them into adjacent rooms and out again into the streets of whatever city it was that convention had pulled us to; Mike Rose, feeling something like I'm feeling, here in this hallway.

As I begin drafting this essay, I've completed another Zoom session with one of my basic writing students. Each time we enter this space, the student is sitting in the same room. A bedpost stands at one corner of the frame; the walls look stark, tall. The student angles his camera in a way that situates him at the very bottom of my monitor, making the walls seem even larger. During the end of our first meeting, I could hear the battery alarm on his smoke detector. Eleven Zoom sessions later, the alarm still randomly pierces our conversations. I imagine that in some future session, I'll open my laptop to find his room on fire. When I share this concern with my student, he tells me he doesn't even hear the alarm any more. Because of health issues, he cannot venture up any ladders; he is waiting for one of his parents to change the battery, as they've promised to do.

This student regularly schedules meetings with me to compensate for absences and to discuss his difficulties with coursework. Born and raised in this working-class steel town, he tells me again and again, "I'm confused." Plumbing his confusion, as Mike Rose would advise, the student and I come to agree he is not confused because he lacks knowledge (*Lives* 236); the assignments confuse him because he does have ways of knowing, ways that often conflict with what I assume to be givens. He brings to class his definitions of "revision," of "outline," of "proposal." They're not the same as mine. I bring up the etymology of "confuse," and we talk about ways his confusion helps me "bring to ruin" the tale I'd predetermined, the curriculum developed before he could even find his desk in our classroom. I indicate to him changes in phrasing I'm now making to our department's standard syllabus in light of his confusion, in light of *our* confusion. Weeks ago, I'd started to smile whenever he began sentences with "I'm confused"; now, when he tells me he's confused, he smiles too.

This student, Mike Rose, and me in this hallway: the space becomes center stage alongside what's supposed to be center stage—a course shell, lectern, scholarly publication. Mike helps us see what difficulties writers face because he centralizes this hallway, the "small stuff" that's never really small. "Of course, big things are important," he says, "curriculum, and pedagogy, and professional and political activities beyond the classroom." However, he also values "everyday signs of commitment"—"[t]he teacher who encourages a hesitant question; . . . who spends an extra five minutes in a conference; who checks in with a student who had difficulty with the last assignment" ("Mike"). He meets in hallways working-class and first-gen students and teachers like himself, like me and my student, and others marginalized in mainstream curricular narratives, makes hallways a center stage.

Here, we contest the "sense of isolation" that's too often "rooted in the books and lectures that surround us, the very language of the place" (Rose, *Lives* 174). We come to learn that what we desire as central to being is not "the mist and vapor of sleep"; we speak back to that "alien voice" that tells us we don't belong (174), open "big things" (Rose, "Mike") to our new phrasing (Rose, *An Open* 1). Our presence in this place changes this place, changes pasts, forges new futures, new ways of knowing and being, from center stage, here in this hallway. This hallway, this now, this nexus of walls and routes, lecterns and desk chairs, anticipation, affirmation, and doubt: this memory of Mike Rose melds with my student on a Zoom call, the smoke among ruins, the alarm that's not an alarm.

I remember Mike Rose in the hallway outside that convention's grand ballroom. I remember, too, that his keynote there highlighted findings from *The Mind at Work,* where he explains the complex thinking that goes into what might seem simple labor. He relayed these findings to a packed house, a room stuffed with teachers, graduate students, and administrators, at their field's premiere conference, center stage. I gave a talk too that day, and the student, not yet my student, was somewhere that day as well. Here, in this hallway, Mike Rose in the doorframe, we learn where.

Works Cited

Rose, Mike. *An Open Language: Selected Writing on Literacy, Learning, and Opportunity.* Bedford/St. Martin, 2006.
—. *Lives on the Boundary: A Moving Account of the Struggles and Achievements of America's Educationally Underprepared.* Penguin, 1989.
—. "Mike Rose's Blog: The Everyday Gestures of Justice." 11 April, 2018. https://nepc.colorado.edu/blog/everyday-gestures.

John Paul Tassoni is professor of English at Miami University. He has served there as the Director of Liberal Education, Director of College Composition, and Co-Coordinator of the regional campuses' Center for Teaching and Learning. He was the founding co-editor of the academic journal *Open Words: Access and English Studies,* for which Mike Rose served as an editorial board member. John is currently editor-in-chief for the *Journal on Centers for Teaching and Learning.*

Mike Rose: Remediating Academia via Inclusive Pedagogy

Kristy Liles Crawley

Celebrating Mike Rose's contributions to the field of Composition and Rhetoric, this tribute recognizes Rose's examination of the harmful "remedial" label in writing studies, honors his call for prioritizing inclusive pedagogy over correctness, and demonstrates that his call for inclusion maintains its relevance today through PARS, an inclusive pedagogical approach.

> "[I]f we can just do x or y, the problem [remedial education] will be solved—in five years, ten years, or a generation—and higher education will be able to return to its real work." (Rose 599)

Mike Rose illuminates the stigma enveloping multiple marginalized students enrolled in remedial writing courses. In "The Language of Exclusion: Writing Instruction at the University," Rose addresses the disturbing notion of writing as a skill to be mastered, when he discusses the problematic label of remedial. He supplies readers with the following definition of remedial: "To remediate seems to mean to correct errors or fill in gaps in a person's knowledge. The implication is that the material being studied should have been learned during prior education but was not" (593). The definition, infused with the assumption that all students have the same educational background, communicates that students have failed to learn the skills or information needed to succeed. With a diverse student population, it is impossible to make such assumptions. Rose reminds readers of the "dynamic and fluid nature of the educational system" (600). Influenced by race, class, economics, and region, each student's educational background is unique in terms of the high school they attended and the required curriculum in place during a specific time period.

Rose adds to this definition as he makes connections between remedial classes and medical terminology, for students are tested, diagnosed, and treated (595). While being treated, remedial students, set apart from curriculum students, appear as a drain on educational institutions' resources or a distraction that keeps them from focusing solely on research and graduate programs. In most cases, physically separated from their peers to be treated, remedial students resume their prescribed treatment. If cured of their writing ailments, students move forward, but those with untreatable cases often disappear from the academy.

By utilizing a medical metaphor for remedial education, Rose attends to exclusion and erasure. Universities and community colleges' entrance exams and placement tests put ESL students' native tongues, students of color's dialects, and first-generation students' struggles to adapt at odds with higher education's standards. Successful treatment, or eradicating problematic writing, aligns with replacing students' languages with the academy's language. Recognizing academia's exclusion, Rose calls for an inclusive pedagogy by reimagining the function and place of writing studies within the academy: "Consider, though, the message that would be sent to the schools and to the society at large if the university embraced—not just financially but conceptually—the teaching of writing: if we gave it full status, championed its rich relationship with inquiry, insisted on the importance of craft and grace, incorporated it into the heart of our curriculum" (602). Along with moving writing away from the margins of the academy, Rose prioritizes inquiry instead of correctness.

Rose's 1985 call for inclusion maintains its relevance today as I work alongside my rhetoric and composition colleagues to interrogate racist and sexist practices to remediate academia, as opposed to students, and enact an inclusive pedagogy. Questions related to race, gender, class, and accessibility have prompted me over the years to move toward an inclusive model of pedagogy hinged on accessibility as opposed to correctness. I utilize Jessie Borgman and Casey McArdle's PARS approach in *Personal, Accessible, Responsive, Strategic: Resources and Strategies for Online Writing Instructors*. Although Borgman and McArdle focus on online instruction, their PARS approach also applies to face-to-face, hybrid, and hyflex classrooms.

Below I illustrate my use of PARS as an inclusive approach to teaching. Due to space limitations, I focus on accessibility in the PARS approach while drawing on my experience with teaching first-year college students who are often diverse students in terms of age, race, gender, and social class. Borgman and McArdle expand the definition of accessibility beyond providing accessible, ADA compliant materials by stating, "Accessible instruction is about more than setting expectations and making you and your course materials accessible to your students, it's also about creating a community of inclusion in your course and inviting students with all levels of ability to interact with you in a way that works for them" (40). Borgman and McArdle's emphasis on building an inclusive community containing students of "all levels of ability" aligns with Rose's rejection of isolation and remediation for students lacking skills or knowledge in their prior education (40). As illustrated in my example below, accessibility plays an important role in helping first-generation college students who often lack experience decoding the language of academia, utilizing technology, and adjusting to their new roles as college students.

Applying Borgman and McArdle's definition above, I will point to a brief example of accessibility. Prior to using PARS, I simply listed a brief description of the writing center's services along with a link to the appointment form on my course syllabus. I soon discovered during one-on-one conferences with students that the brief description left many students with more questions than answers. When I attempted to uncover some of my students' reluctance to visit the writing center, students shared with me their thoughts. Associating tutoring with expensive SAT prep and professional for-profit tutoring centers, one student mentioned that he could not afford their services while another student equated the writing center's services to their previous after-school experience in high school involving test or paper corrections and extra credit assignments for failing students in their English class. Students' past experiences shaped their attitudes toward my tutoring recommendations as well as exemplified financial barriers and systemic racism in education. First-generation students, often nonwhite and from lower socioeconomic backgrounds, frequently attend underfunded high schools that lack essential tutoring services. Such barriers contribute to their potential continued struggles in college.

My conversations with students prompted me to apply a PARS approach. Revising my syllabus, I provided links to a Q&A as well as demonstrated through a video the process of making an appointment online. For synchronous and face-to-face classes, I invited writing center tutors as guest speakers to supply students with further details about their services. For asynchronous online classes, I created a recording of these details to post. The instructional video allowed students to hear my voice as well as see the process of navigating through multiple areas of the writing center's website. This approach took into account students' learning styles (auditory, visual, kinesthetic, etc.), as well as differing levels of writing center knowledge and technology experience when introducing them to the writing center.

After implementing changes in my approach to making accessible materials, I noticed students' comprehension of the writing center's services changed in their understanding of the writing center as a space for dialogue and learning. Some alluded to their sense of belonging through preferences in working with specific tutors and their plans for future tutoring sessions. Personal conferences in addition to surveys and informal Zoom polls functioned as a means for me to continue gauging students' success in accessing services and allowing them to communicate their needs.

As I reflect on this example from my own teaching utilizing PARS, Rose's call for methods of support and inclusion rather than exclusion and remediation continues to resonate. Rose continues to influence today's scholars by shifting educators' interpretations of students' needs. Instead of students' needs being a source of deficiency, their needs are a foundation for building a network of support through accessible resources, peers, tutors, educators, and college services.

WORKS CITED

Borgman, Jessie, and Casey McArdle. *Personal, Accessible, Responsive, Strategic: Resources and Strategies for Online Writing Instructors.* WAC Clearinghouse, 2019.

Rose, Mike. "The Language of Exclusion: Writing Instruction at the University." *The Norton Book of Composition Studies.* edited by Susan Miller, W.W. Norton & Company, 2009, pp. 586-604.

Kristy Liles Crawley is professor of English at Forsyth Technical Community College in Winston-Salem, North Carolina. Her research on pedagogy and rhetorical studies appears in *Prose Studies*; *Peitho: Journal of the Coalition of Feminist Scholars in the History of Rhetoric and Composition*; *Teaching English in the Two-Year College*; *Routledge Companion to Literature and Class*; *PARS in Practice: More Resources and Strategies for Online Writing Instructors*; and *Teachers, Teaching, and Media: Original Essays about Educators and Popular Culture.*

Reminding Us Why We Are Here: Mike Rose's Legacy for Basic Writing

Lynn Reid

In this essay, the author explores why, over a career that spanned more than four decades, Mike Rose frequently critiqued existing conceptions of remediation. Rather than calling for its elimination, the author argues Rose challenged teacher-scholars to reimagine our work to provide support for students whose academic experiences prior to college did not put them on equal footing with their peers.

Any WPA who specializes in or oversees courses that carry a designation of "remedial" has likely spent a fair amount of time defending the work of basic writing courses to institutional stakeholders who are far-removed from the day-to-day classroom experience of many basic writing instructors. Today, remedial courses are increasingly targeted for elimination, blamed for slowing progress toward degrees, reinforcing institutional racism, and discouraging students who might be better placed in a traditional credit-bearing FYC course. While all of this can be (and is often) true, a look back at Rose's work on remediation provides another view, one that reminds us all that for some students, remedial courses in reading and writing offer a necessary–and, indeed, sometimes the only–pathway to accessing higher education.

To help explain to faculty and administrators beyond the writing program the level of instruction that students enrolled in remedial courses might actually need, I find myself turning often to Rose's "Time to Help College Professors Be Better Teachers," published about a decade ago in *The Christian Science Monitor*. In this brief article, Rose argues that more than anything, what colleges need to support nontraditional students or students who might carry the institutional label of academically "at-risk" is a renewed emphasis on *teaching*. In this brief article, Rose provides the guidance that I could have used myself when I was a new instructor. He opens with a simple example of a classroom activity:

> Right after I gave my opening lecture on Oedipus the King to the 30 employees of Los Angeles's criminal justice system, I handed out a few pages of notes I would have taken if I were sitting in their seats listening to the likes of me…we spent the last half hour of the class comparing my notes with the ones they had just taken, talking about

the way I signaled that something was important, how they could separate out a big idea from specific facts, how to ask a question without looking like a dummy. (Rose)

Those few sentences elegantly capture so many facets of basic writing instruction: the need for explicit *teaching* through modeling, the benefits of metacognition from the comparison between a model and student's own work, the importance of teaching students how to recognize the subtle cues in a lecture that signal emphasis, and how to walk the fine line that acknowledges what students need to learn about how to succeed as learners, regardless of the topic at hand, without making them feel badly about not already knowing it. These are the elements of basic writing instruction that are too often obscured in contemporary discourse about remediation.

Rose certainly identified problems with traditional models of remediation throughout his career as he argued for a shift away from grammatically-correct prose and toward a vision for *learning* that made room for a range of linguistic backgrounds, personal experience, academic inquiry, and messy attempts at engaging complexity ("Remedial Writing Courses: A Critique and a Proposal"). While he provided necessary critiques to remediation, Rose stopped short of calling for its elimination. Instead, much of his work rested on how we could better serve students who had been underserved before college and those whose academic journeys have been disrupted by circumstances beyond their control. Mike Rose saw the writing on the wall: eliminating courses that are labeled as "remedial" does not eliminate the learning needs of students who would have enrolled in those courses. Instead, eliminating those courses and the associated professional expertise renders the needs of those students invisible within larger institutional systems.

What's unique about Mike Rose's contribution to basic writing studies is his explicit effort to explain our work to people outside of the discipline, knowing too well that these external audiences would have a hand in determining the future of remediation. In *Why School?*, another piece written for a popular audience, Rose writes, "There have to be mechanisms in an educational system as vast and complex and flawed as ours to remedy the system's failures. Rather than marginalizing remediation, colleges should invest more intellectual resources into it, making it as serious and effective as it can be" (9). Here, as in many of his other works, Rose captures the tension that teacher-scholars who work in basic writing negotiate every day: acknowledging the role of our courses in both reinforcing existing inequities in higher education and also simultaneously providing instruction for the metacognitive strategies for reading and writing that are not immediately obvious to all students.

At its core, Rose's body of work on remediation demands that his readers *see* the lived experiences of students and teachers in basic writing, reminding us all that simply turning away from this work will not create an inherently equitable environment for all students. We know that students are effective communicators in their own right, yet their college courses and professional goals may demand communication that is different from what they know. We know that students can work with complex ideas from the start of their academic journeys, yet they may struggle with comprehension and abstraction. We know that placing students in courses with a basic skills designation can serve to marginalize them, yet without those courses, students who need additional support may struggle to find it. We know that focusing on cognition can be reductive, yet students who have experienced poverty and racism are more likely to bear the effects of trauma that impact cognition and learning.

Among Mike Rose's most important legacies is his constant reminder to lean into these tensions in order to ensure that they remain visible to stakeholders within and beyond our institutions. Rose envisioned a transformative future rooted in interdisciplinary research across methodologies for courses that have historically served students that are deemed least prepared for higher education ("Remediation at the Crossroads"). For as much as Mike Rose critiqued remediation, the spotlight that he held on these courses for more than four decades reminds us that we should be focused on how to do it better rather than to simply not do it at all.

Works Cited

Rose, Mike. "Remediation at the Crossroads." *Inside Higher Ed.*, 21 April 2011, https://www.insidehighered.com/views/2011/04/21/remediation-crossroads

—. "Remedial Writing Courses: A Critique and a Proposal." *College English*, vol. 45, no. 2, National Council of Teachers of English, 1983, pp. 109–28, https://doi.org/10.2307/377219.

—. "Time to Help College Professors Be Better Teachers." *Christian Science Monitor*, 22Mar2013https://www.csmonitor.com/Commentary/Opinion/2013/0322/Time-to-help-college-professors-be-better-teachers

—. *Why School? Reclaiming Education for All of Us*. The New Press, 2009.

Lynn Reid is assistant professor of rhetoric and composition and university director of basic writing at Fairleigh Dickinson University. She has served as the co-chair for the Council on Basic Writing, a CCCC Standing Group and is co-editing a special issue of *Journal of Basic Writing* focused on legacies of Open Admissions. Her work has appeared in *JBW, WPA Journal, Kairos, TESOL Journal*, and several edited collections.

Once You're Seen You Can't Unsee

Christina Saidy

This contribution describes the way that Mike Rose weaved story, research, and commentary, and challenged us to question simple counting as a way to understand readiness, competence, and literacy and to see student writers deeply. Rose's work continues to have deep implications for the work of WPAs and writing teacher/scholars.

The first time I read Mike Rose's *Lives on the Boundary* I could not put it down. Like Rose, I grew up in the Los Angeles area. I was the child of working-class parents. My father, an immigrant from Brazil, worked in food service, and my mother, a white woman whose family transplanted from Detroit to Southern California in the late 1950s, was a medical technician. Like Rose's parents, my parents "had heard that quality schooling meant private, Catholic schooling, so they somehow got the money together" to send me to Catholic school (Rose 23).

In 1994, I ended up at UCLA and I was completely out of my league. As a first-generation student, I felt deeply that the university was not for students like me, and, without any institutional understanding, I assumed this was a personal shortcoming. Fortunately, I was a student in the Academic Advancement Program (AAP), the program Rose called EOP. I spent my years at UCLA immersed in the culture of learning in Campbell Hall, first as a student attending tutoring and then as a tutor in the Humanities Lab. Campbell Hall was constantly abuzz with learning. There were days when we could not even find a table in the humanities lab, so we would sit on the floor, or when the tutoring group was so big that we had to move outside to the patio. It was in Campbell Hall that I learned about being a writer in community with other writers. As AAP tutors, we had to meet with the professors teaching the classes we were tutoring. I went to meet with the professor of English 10A -- the first part of the British Literature series. As we sat in his office, he sincerely lectured me about "those AAP students" and their deficits. When he stopped, I said "I am an AAP student. I look forward to helping my peers with your class." His look taught me so much about the way that deficit thinking is about the failure to see students.

In many ways, Rose's *Lives* was ahead of its time, as if Rose were preparing us for the reality of the neo-liberal university. In it, Rose questioned the ways we measure literacy, noting, "When in doubt or when scared or when pressed, count" (209). Rose called out counting as a lazy way to understand readiness, competence, and literacy. He argued, "our basic orientations toward the teaching and testing of literacy contribute to our inability to see" and he saw the stories in *Lives* as a way to "encourage us to sit close by as people use language and consider, as we listen, the orientations that limit our field of vision" (205).

To help us see, Mike Rose wove story with research and commentary masterfully, and it was the story that often stood out. I have never forgotten the UCLA dean who Mike Rose wrote about in "The Language of Exclusion" who "referred to students in remedial English as 'the truly illiterate among us'" (352). Rose told the story of that dean so we both understand Rose's facts and argument and so that we would remember when we make administrative choices, we are making them about students, not numbers. Rose made sure we would never forget Mr. MacFarland, the teacher who changed Rose's relationship with literacy and with schooling. He told that story to remind us of the potential for teachers to effect change and to remind us that "students will float to the mark you set" (*Lives 26*). In *Lives*, Rose told the stories of Laura and Bobby set against the stark contrast of his description of the UCLA campus where the affluence "hits you most forcefully at lunchtime" (3) so that we see what Laura and Bobby might see and why Bobby might say, "We don't belong at UCLA, do we?" (4). As Rose told these stories of others, so too he told own story of accessing school and the university. Rose laid bare the challenges of schooling and academic life in a way that is honest and that most of us had never read before up to that point.

It is no wonder I felt seen by Rose's method of weaving story, research, and commentary. It is because in his scholarship Mike Rose challenged us to question simple counting and to look and see deeply. Rose's work continues to have deep implications for the work of WPAs and writing teachers and scholars. Programmatically, we should question the counting that we use to evaluate and sort students, especially students who may be labeled unprepared. In my article for this journal (2018), I recommend using case studies to better see and understand the students in our programs, rather than counting to sort and label. In teaching, we want to deeply understand our students and the rich literacies they bring with them to the university. Most semesters, I use snippets from chapter two of *Lives* to inspire students in telling their literacy histories and stories. As they respond to Rose's stories with their own, I learn to see them and their literacies. As a scholar, though, Rose has encouraged me most to bring stories into my scholarship. There is pressure in the field to move away from story to legitimize our research. But it is important to focus our research around the stories of those who are often unseen in order to *expand* our field of vision.

I started this vignette with my story so you might see me and understand a time in my life when I felt unseen as a writer and learner. The legacy of Mike Rose's work is that through story we learn to see deeply. This continues to have profound implications for the many layers of our work: programmatic, teaching, research. When we center story, we can see the things we might miss about writers if we simply count.

Works Cited

Rose, Mike. *Lives on the Boundary.* New York: Penguin Books, 1990.

—. "The Language of Exclusion: Writing Instruction in the University." *College English* 47.4 (1985): 341-359.

Saidy, Christina. "Inez in Transition: Using Case Study to Explore the Experiences of Underrepresented Students in First-Year Composition." *Writing Program Administration* 41.2 (2018): 17-35.

Christina Saidy is associate professor of English at Arizona State University. Her research focuses on writing and writing transitions with secondary students, teachers in professional development groups, and students entering college. Christina's work has appeared in journals such as *English Journal, College Composition and Communication, WPA: Writing Program Administration, Teaching/Writing,* and *Teaching English in the Two-Year College.*

Lives in the Complexity

Douglas Hesse

Mike Rose's early teaching and writing administration, reflected in conversations and documents from the late 1970's to early 1990s, use pragmatic cognitivist frameworks to further progressive goals. While he modified and recontextualized this framework as he became an elder statesman and public intellectual, he maintained these views. The author asserts, from Rose's life and career, contemporary WPAs might take three lessons: Write regularly, including for personal interests, not only disciplinary fealty; Value identities as teachers and writers as equal to administrative advancement; Practice passions kindly.

"Okay, but can he write?"[1]

I first met Mike Rose in March 1994, when he gave a talk at Illinois State, where I was directing the writing program. We were using his textbook with Malcolm Kiniry, *Critical Strategies for Academic Thinking and Writing*, and Bedford/St. Martin's agreed to send him to Normal. We were happy enough to hear about pedagogy but more interested in meeting the author of *Lives on the Boundary* and essays like "Rigid Rules, Inflexible Plans, and the Stifling of Language" that were mainstays of the TA teaching seminar.

I have just a couple impressions from that distant encounter. Neither involves remarks on the textbook, which are lost to me. Instead, I remember Mike's interest in my own working-class past, the first-gone-to-college son of a garbage truck driver and a homemaker. That connection, fueled by his basic kindness, kept us in touch over the years. Mind you, we were hardly close friends, and no doubt hundreds of others enjoyed what I did: Mike chatting when we crossed paths, asking about family, sharing recent experiences and ideas. Occasionally, I'd get a note, often tied to new publications, but the promotional part of such messages was apologetic. The other impression—and I'm hesitant to share it, doing so only because later I joked about it with Mike himself—was that a few students and colleagues told me how good looking they found him. Thirty-something me didn't know what to do with such comments. Sixty-something me looks back through foggy lenses and smiles.

By the time we met, Mike was balancing identities from two different but related sources: a cognitivist paradigm grounded in psychology and a genre paradigm grounded in discourse theory. I recognized the first, represented by *Writer's Block: The Cognitive Dimension*, as important but, I'll confess, not personally interesting. My failure. I found the second keenly interesting. This work, which recognized discursive differences among academic disciplines and intellectual operations they shared, appealed because it solved curricular and pedagogical problems for those of us then directing large writing programs.

What I wasn't fully recognizing in 1994 was what would become Rose's most important identity: as narrative chronicler of literate lives of individuals who didn't track the "traditional" (aka white middle-class) mainstream. Yes, there was the groundbreaking *Lives on the Boundary*. But as strange as it might now seem today, thirty years ago it seemed something of a fortunate aberration. When Annie Dillard published her shimmering essay collection *Teaching a Stone to Talk*, she included an "Author's Note" that explained in part, "At any rate, this is not a collection of occasional pieces, such as a writer brings out to supplement his real work; instead this is my real work, such as it is" (vi). *Lives* was Mike's real work. Or at least part of it.

He cheerfully tried to reconcile his scholarly interests as he grew into an elder statesman. His 2006 collection, *An Open Language: Selected Writing on Literacy, Learning, and Opportunity*, reflects on conflicts between his cognitivist orientation and the social critiques that were impugning its assumptions. He noted that he still saw in cognition "a democratic possibility and a critical vocabulary" (13). Rose accounted for individuals operating within social formations, modifying his work as did Pat Bizzell--her own cognitive confidence in *Academic Discourse and Critical Consciousness*. He focused most consistently on class, with the *scene* of this focus, to invoke Burke's term, first the school, later the workplace. The organization of *An Open Language* is revealing in terms of the time-overlapped section headings under that organize the book's twenty-eight chapters:

> The Cognition of Composing, 1980-1985
>
> Teaching Academic Writing, 1979-2001
>
> Integrating the Cognitive and the Social Critical Perspectives on Writing Instruction, 1985-1991
>
> School and Society, 1989-1995
>
> The Mind at Work: Researching the Everyday, 1999-2004
>
> Public Writing: Style and Persuasion, 1989-2005

Re-reading the collection's preface and introductions, I appreciate Mike candidly confessing limitations, especially in method even as he defends his corpus, and arguing its coherence. I've done probably 75-80 external reviews for tenure and promotion, and I always pause at the direction, inevitably from research universities, to assess both the prominence and coherence of research agendas. In part, this manifests the anxious defense of disciplinarity, which wants systematic methods applied to bounded questions. The threatening counter-practice is journalism, professors exploring opportunistic subjects through narrative approaches for audiences that may, heaven forbid, include general readers. Mike increasingly turned that direction, doubling down on the approach of *Lives on the Boundary* or *The Mind at Work*. While I don't think it crucial to define Mike Rose's research agenda, if pressed, I'd point to the urgent, eloquent desire to understand literate practice in all its individual complexities, providing practical approaches to penetrate barriers and misperceptions.

Mike's public turn brought deserved attention and respect both within our field and beyond, ultimately generating recognition such as *The New Yorker's* posthumous appreciation (Dettmar). We surely might heed his call "to bring research and practice into the public sphere, both to test and refine them and to seek broader influence" ("An Open" 9). I think our profession has gotten a little better in the dozen years since he wrote, but his observation still holds:

> We academics easily develop a tin ear to the sound of our own language. We talk too much to each other, and not beyond. We risk linguistic, intellectual, and political isolation. Many good things have come of rhetoric and compositions move toward disciplinary status. But with disciplinarity also comes a turn inward, a concentration on the mechanics of the profession, on internal debates and intellectual display. . . . ("Writing" 291)

While it might seem regressive, I want to explore the early research that brought him to Normal, scholarship grounded in both practical and intellectual interests. Early on, Mike (like many of us), had administrative responsibilities as part of the formidable group at UCLA in the late seventies/early eighties, which included Carol Hartzog as Director of Writing Programs and Richard Lanham as Executive Director. By the mid 1980s, he was Director of the UCLA first-year program, and his 1984 "Descriptive Report" is instructive. Take the report's first curricular principle: "Writing must be taught as a vital process that aids the storing, structuring, discovering, and re-visioning of information for self and others, a process central to our attempts to make sense of the world" (11). There's a striking emphasis on information over rhetoric, on writing as an epistemic act. Or take the second principle: "University students must learn to write the kind of discourse that is central to academic inquiry" (11) and the related third: "When possible, writing assignments should be built on the kinds of materials students encounter at the university" (12). The document conservatively positions the first-year course as academic discourse as opposed, say, to civic or vocational.

Rose's role required shepherding a *teachable* curriculum for TA's. It had to have a discernible logic and direction, assignments and methods both meaningful and doable. Simultaneously, the curriculum had to assuage a wider university community that expected value in a required *writing* course. Certainly, communal expectations could be misguided, and Rose and colleagues pushed back against servile "correctness," for example. The UCLA curricular principles were ambitious, absolutely, but they kept steadily to developing skills *in* writing rather than, say, inculcating ideas *about* writing, or about wider issues and problems. There were six course options.

- "A Course in Autobiography—From Personal to Academic Writing" was informed by the Bartholomae/Petrosky *Ways of Knowing* sequence to move students from writing autobiographies, to analyzing classmates' writings, to abstracting larger principles (22).
- "The Freshman Preparatory Program Curriculum" applied specific cognitive strategies to materials and problems from different disciplines (23).
- "The Project Workshop" functioned as a lab/seminar where students complete three or four projects requiring extensive research, choosing from instructor-provided lists (26).
- "The Cross-Disciplinary Theme-Centered Course" had students write from texts on a central theme treated in multiple disciplines (Rose uses the example of "Insiders and Outsiders," with texts from literature, sociology, and biology). The theme is meant to be a vehicle for developing strategies for academic writing, not a destination (24).
- "Cross-Cultural Readings Curriculum" courses used "fiction from Central and Latin America, Asia, and Africa" alongside readings from "political science, anthropology, history, sociology, and psychology." Rose explicitly asserted "this is not a literature course, but rather a writing course that builds assignments from literary and social science texts" (25).
- "Introduction to Academic Reading Writing: The History of Ideas Format." This emphasis, designed for developing students, was "built on key issues or figures in Western intellectual history" from religion, philosophy, science, politics, and art (25).

Rose's sixty-page report includes sample syllabi and other materials (for example, a two-hour placement test that has students read a passage from Studs Terkel's *Working* and write from one of three prompts). Looking at the document through the eyes of a longtime WPA, I'm struck by two things. I recognize, first, a certain element of appeasement, a desire to accommodate different teaching interests within the program—and different interests/pressures beyond it. But, second, Rose and his colleagues sought to provide a map and legend through higher ed's strange landscape by focusing on finite strategies. Which?

One of Rose's earliest publications was "Teaching University Discourse: A Theoretical Framework and a Curriculum," presented at a meeting of the Canadian Council of Teachers of English. The paper explains that "the freshman composition course must bridge faculty expectations and student skill" through five components of exposition: seriation, classification, synthesis, compare/contrast, and analysis.

Those strategies later transmuted into defining, summarizing, serializing, classifying, comparing, and analyzing. This might seem like the stuff of current-traditional rhetoric. It's not. Rather than providing models for mimicry, *Critical Strategies* poses analytic questions and structured processes, with informal writing-to-learn activities along the way. There's extensive how-to advice and plenty of cases from different disciplines. The chapter on definition, for example, includes issues from political science and psychology, among others, and has writing options from biology, genetics, history, philosophy, and others. Unlike WID efforts that would have students emulate specific disciplinary discourse conventions (although Appendix 2 does scaffold "Exploring the Discourse of Your Major") and unlike thematic foci whose content ever threaten to sideline writing itself, Kiniry and Rose try building writerly synapses through cognitive operations.

With a disciplinary dissecting microscope of twenty-five years, I could readily call out reductive assumptions in the long-ago UCLA program. I could question whether academic discourse (not civic or cultural) is the best focus for required writing. I suspect Mike could, too. But what impresses me still is how these courses are *in* writing, not *about* it—or about any host of extra-writing agendas. At a time when [outlandish claim alert] we organize so much writing instruction to indulge our own theories of language, identity, and authority, at a time when decades of research and theory have rightly rendered writing and its development impossibly complex, WPAs might take a lesson from Mike. We might see students as individuals differently inhabiting the world, not as representatives of categories or classifications.

WPAs might take three more lessons.

1. Write. "But," we might protest, "we do!" Certainly, we produce the multiple kinds of instrumental writing needed to do our jobs, much of it evanescent and obliged. We do scholarship beyond instructions and reports, reviews and policies—all kinds of activities Mike would perhaps regard as connecting us with the workers he championed. But Mike enacted other kinds of writing, much of it closer to journalism than ethnography, welling from observation and conversation, for readers who want to read as well as those simply obliged, in genres where narrative and scene matter as much as analysis. Such writing might advance our professional cause publicly, yes, but it might as importantly make ourselves more fully Our Selves, with what and how we write shaped by personal interests rather than dictated by disciplinary fealty. Read his poem about Richard Brautigan ("He Used"). Perhaps to do this writing we might do less of others.

2. Value our identity as teachers and writers. While some of us fall into WPA work by circumstance, others increasingly pursue it by design. (See endnote 2.) That's fine, of course, and no doubt being WPA brings rewards intellectual and financial. But being a WPA can become a dazzling, consumptive identity. More power to those who relish that identity and want to climb ladders. But demurring is not failure. I simply assert the nobility of being teacher and writer, professional identities beyond "manager" that brought us to the field. I hope. At some point, Mike stopped being WPA, and his most influential work arguably happened then. I'm a fine hypocrite to say so, but it's reasonable to leave WPA work for something that may be more rewarding and important. It was for Mike.

3. Practice passions kindly. Mike certainly aspired to ideas and experiences, partly I'm sure for ego's reasons that impel us all. But there was also the imperative, embraced as responsibility, to improve lives of people who don't get a fair shake. Along the way, he took time with others, especially listening to them, not just pressing his agenda. Perhaps his working-class background bred kindness as coping. Regardless of our personal pasts, we can all aspire to be counted kind.

Figure 1. Inscription from Mike Rose to Doug Hesse

Notes

1. The epigraph is a question posed by editors to Mike Rose's agent, who was trying to sell *Lives on the Boundary*. It was motivated by skepticism of professors' abilities to reach publics. ("Writing for the Public," p. 284).

2. I write about these developments in Hesse, Douglas. "Aging Through the Thirty-Year Rise of Professionalized Writing Administration." *Talking Back: Senior Scholars and Their Colleagues Deliberate the Past, Present, and Future of Writing Studies*, edited by Norbert Elliot and Alice Horning, U Colorado P, 2020, pp. 189-209.

Works Cited

Bizzell, Patricia. *Academic Discourse and Critical Consciousness*. U Pittsburgh P, 1992.

Dettmar, Kevin. "The Teacher Who Changed How We Teach Writing." *The New Yorker*, 14 Oct. 2021, https://www.newyorker.com/culture/postscript/the-teacher-who-changed-how-we-teach-writing

Dillard, Annie. *Teaching a Stone to Talk: Expeditions and Encounters*. Harper Colophon, 1983.

Kiniry, Malcolm and Mike Rose, *Critical Strategies for Academic Thinking and Writing, Compact Second Edition*. Bedford/St. Martin's, 1995.

Rose, Mike. *An Open Language: Selected Writing on Literacy, Learning, and Opportunity*. Bedford/St. Martins, 2006.

—. *The Freshman Writing Program: A Descriptive Report*. Eric Document 247 567, 1984.

—. "He Used Sweet Wine in Place of Life Because He Didn't Have Any More Life to Use." *College English*, vol 47, no. 6, 1985, p. 610

—. *Lives on the Boundary: The Struggles and Achievements of America's Underprepared*. Free Press, 1989.

—. *The Mind at Work: Valuing the Intelligence of the American Worker*. Penguin, 2014.

—. "Rigid Rules, Inflexible Plans, and the Stifling of Language" A Cognitivist Analysis of Writer's Block." *CCC*, vol. 31, no. 4, 1980, pp. 389-401.

—. "Teaching University Discourse: Theoretical Framework and a Curriculum." Canadian Council of Teachers of English, Ottawa, May 1979. ERIC Document 173 784, 1979.

—. "Writing for the Public." *College English*, vol. 72, no. 3, 2010, pp. 284-292.

Doug Hesse is professor of writing at the University of Denver, where he has been named University Distinguished Scholar and where he served as founding executive director of the writing program. He is currently chair of AWAC and is a former president of NCTE, former chair of CCCC, former president of the CWPA, former editor of *WPA: Writing Program Administration*, and former chair of the MLA Division on Teaching. Hesse is author of over 90 essays, essays, and book chapters. He's co-author of four books, with a fifth forthcoming. His scholarly interests are creative nonfiction, writing pedagogy and administration, and writing as craft in a field of craft/artisanal work. He sings semi-professionally.

Encountering Lives on the Boundary: Mike Rose as Methodologist for Centering Minoritized Writers

Ray Rosas

This essay considers how Mike Rose's work might be taken up to advance antiracist writing program administration. Throughout his career, Rose centered the experiences of minoritized writers through a variety of naturalistic methods. The author contends that Rose's equity-driven, emic-oriented research contributions provide a generative resource for emerging antiracist work.

I attend graduate school about forty-minutes east of Mike Rose's hometown of Altoona, Pennsylvania. Although it's difficult to explain, this fact is somehow a source of comfort and encouragement. As a Latino, first-generation college student from a working-class background, I learned quickly to identify the scholars and researchers who have my back, the scholars and researchers who support what I do and who do their best to make academe a livable environment for outsiders like me. Though I was not lucky enough to have met Rose, his work assured me that he had my back. And knowing that this early champion of minoritized writers grew up just "down the street" from where I live remains a source of personal comfort, however difficult that comfort is to verbalize.

I highlight this personal experience to gesture towards what I believe is the abiding element, the epistemological epicenter of Rose's distinguished oeuvre: his use of naturalistic methods to center the lived experiences of writers minoritized by culture, race, socioeconomic class, or education. Whether through stimulated recall protocols, ethnographic case studies, autobiographical narratives, or, of course, classroom observations, Rose coupled method to a research agenda concerned with making academe more accessible and equitable—less entrenched in its "club" mentality with its glitzy badges, opaque language, and worship of tradition (Rose 58). Rose's classic classroom study with Glynda Hull, Kay Losey Fraser, and Marisa Castellano is illustrative on this point. Recall that this study highlighted the lived experience of Maria, a precocious first-year writer who, internalizing the negative feedback from her instructor in classroom conversation, comes to define herself as having "some problems with . . . English" (Hull et al. 317). This study united traditional classroom observations with critical discourse analysis (CDA) and interviews to uncover the micro-interactional politics of classroom discourse and make recommendations for programmatic reform as well as teacher development. In short, this study deployed a robust methodological framework to provide emic understanding of the myriad ways microaggressions manifest in classroom talk. As readers of this work, we become privy to the unfortunate but common process of minoritization in the writing classroom (through observations and CDA) and its toll on Maria's sense of self-worth (through interview data).

I stress the underlying methods of the above study because it is perhaps easy to overlook Rose's legacy as a methodologist. After all, we remember the outcomes of research more than the means of achieving them. There are many Marias in Rose's long list of publications: first-year and early-career writers that find themselves pitted against and undermined by hegemonic literacy practices and unstated discourse norms. Rose not only pinpointed such practices but also showed us how to remediate ourselves—our institutions, our writing programs, our classrooms, our attitudes—in ways that make for more accessible and equitable educational experiences. Underlying all this generative work was a commitment to the emic, to using naturalistic methods to understand the lived experiences of lives on the boundary.

Although we can certainly celebrate the impact of Rose's work in the areas of access, accessibility, and socioeconomic equity, I want to point to the ways Rose's work might be taken up to advance antiracist writing program administration. Staci M. Perryman-Clark and Collin Lamont Craig demonstrate "how making race visible in our intersecting administrative and curricular practices creates opportunities to both explore and problematize writing program administration as a framework for institutional and disciplinary critique" (1). And Mya Poe reminds us that analysis of race and racism must be localized if we hope to glean actionable insight for programmatic and curricular reform (5). In my view, the viability of the antiracist turn in writing program administration demands attention to the emic. Such a turn demands an intentional use of naturalistic methods to tap the insights and lived experiences of the many stakeholders affected by writing program administration, especially the insights and lived experiences of minoritized students.

Attention to the emic is critical because making race visible presents numerous methodological challenges. Experiences of race and racism are neither static nor monolithic, and writing researchers and WPAs cannot assume that formal educational contexts operate as the only or most salient context in which race and racism become activated for any one individual. As Walter R. Allen contends, the problems faced by minoritized students in educational contexts are symptomatic of "larger systemic problems" (42). Thus, writing researchers and WPAs who delineate contexts of race and racism narrowly are missing out on the much wider racial picture. Access to the wider racial picture, furthermore, can be achieved through careful attention to the ways informants—research participants—narrate their literacy experiences as raced individuals. By listening to *their* perspectives, writing researchers and WPAs can develop deeper, more holistic understandings of what it means to write from the racialized subaltern.

Rose knew that only a holistic approach to literacy would yield actionable insight, which is why he worked tirelessly to explicate all "the complex ties between literacy and culture" (8). As showcased in Hull et al. and more recently in *Why School?: Reclaiming Education for All of Us*, the writers at the core of Rose's research and social commentary are rarely one-dimensional. Instead, they are multidimensional, historically situated individuals who illustrate the range of literate experience from anxious and frustrating writing performances to confident and triumphant ones. Rose's life work, then, entailed the creation of granular, nuanced tapestries of literate experience; such tapestries undergirded his calls for educational equity.

Emerging antiracist work needs detailed tapestries of literate experience to support both broad and nuanced antiracist efforts. In this respect, Rose's brand of equity-driven, emic-oriented research provides a generative model for the work ahead. Ultimately, Mike Rose taught us how to leverage sound methodological protocols for the purpose of social and institutional critique. I believe we can honor and celebrate Rose's legacy by borrowing his union of method and equity-driven telos to advance our visions of antiracist writing program administration; I believe we can honor and celebrate Rose's work by making visible the context-specific ways writing program administrators can clear the way for minoritized writers to move from the boundaries of academe to the center.

Works Cited

Allen, Walter R., et al. *College in Black and White: African American Students in Predominantly White and in Historically Black Public Universities.* State University of New York Press, 1991.

Hull, Glynda, et al. "Remediation as Social Construct: Perspectives from an Analysis of Classroom Discourse." *College Composition and Communication*, vol. 42, no. 3, 1991, pp. 299-329.

Perryman-Clark, Staci, and Collin L. Craig. *Black Perspectives in Writing Program Administration: From the Margins to the Center.* National Council of Teachers of English, 2019.

Poe, Mya. "Re-framing Race in Teaching Writing Across the Curriculum." *Across the Disciplines*, vol.10, no. 3, 2013, pp.1-14.

Rose, Mike. *Lives on the Boundary: The Struggles and Achievements of America's Underprepared.* Free Press, 1989.

—. *Why School?: Reclaiming Education for All of Us.* New Press, 2009.

Ray Rosas is a PhD candidate in rhetoric and writing studies at Penn State. His academic interests include critical literacy studies, rhetorical genre studies, and the rhetoric of health and medicine. His dissertation employs a phenomenological research design to study the unique writing strategies of Black and Latinx writers at a predominantly white institution.

Whatever Happened to Average? Heeding Mike Rose's Call

Kelly Ritter

This brief essay puts Mike Rose's Lives on the Boundary in conversation with recent scholarship on socioeconomic disparities present in pre-college credit programs in high schools (specifically Advanced Placement), and the effects these disparities later have on first-year college students who are also first-generation.

As someone whose career has focused on histories of writing, social class, and literacy, I can think of no scholar more important to my own origin story than Mike Rose. In 2014, when I was editor of *College English*, I was fortunate to receive a letter from him, in response to an article we had published by Betsy Bowen and Kathryn Nantz, titled "What is The Value of the GED?". It opened this way:

> O.K., so this is going to be an odd letter, a hybrid form: a fan letter to Betsy and Kathryn and a letter commending Kelly for publishing an article on the GED and, equally important, for publishing an article in College English co-authored by an economist. I'll bet it's the only time in the last half-dozen years that an economist appeared as an author in College English . . .

The letter continued:

> As Betsy and Kathryn point out, we in composition and writing studies don't focus much attention on the population represented in their article. I have heard many similar complaints from people who teach in community college and/or in remedial-basic-developmental writing programs. We're talking about a lot of students, many of whom present significant needs and challenges to our skill and knowledge. We need to be thinking hard about how to help them and how to advocate for them . . .
>
> Why doesn't our field encourage (and create the conditions to make possible) a few of us to become knowledgeable—or collaborate—in both rhetoric and economics, or in statistics and feminist methods, or in teacher research and public policy analysis?

Eight years later, I continue to reflect on the lingering gravity of Rose's words. As Ken Harvey famously laments in *Lives on the Boundary*, "I just wanna be average" (28). Ken longs to eschew "the identity implied in the vocational track . . . [and be] the Common Joe" (29). Yet today, we want students to be anything *but* average. Though we say we celebrate difference, we more typically erase it. We efficiently monetize the high school years so as to bypass the college general education experience, including first-year writing, through accumulation of pre-college credits in various forms (and potentially at inappropriate developmental levels). Right now, the *speed* with which one receives a college degree is more valued than the trajectory *of* that degree, or the *person* earning it. We do not do enough to interrogate how these economic models of higher ed impact our field. For their part, Kristine Hansen and Christine R. Ferris also sounded this warning over a decade ago in their groundbreaking volume on AP, Dual Credit, and Dual Enrollment (*College Credit* 2010). We have yet, however, to heed it.

Our current focus on credentialed pathways has the goal of a homogenized workforce that shudders at the label "average," and has no use for students like Ken, or (ironically) GED recipients who bypassed high school *itself*. When Rose told Ken's story in 1989, AP credit was typically granted to a small number of top students, usually in just one or two subjects. When I graduated in 1987, my 1200 person high school in a midwestern college town had only two AP courses; my daughter's former high school of about the same size—also in a midwestern college town—in 2022 offers AP courses in *20* subjects. And yet, as my daughter has herself observed, the students who enroll in these courses are rarely those from lower socioeconomic classes (and also, are rarely students of color). Even as the College Board claims to be working toward more widespread availability of AP curricula in both urban and rural underserved communities, the fact remains: pre-college experiences are at their root unequal in the United States today, and students who start college lacking the now-standard 12 or more hours of pre-college credit are made to feel *not ready*. AP is now the gold standard, offering "advanced exemption" rather than the original goal of advanced *credit*, to borrow from David Joliffe's important distinctions. Though my own experience was not like Ken's, I was a first-gen, working-class student who struggled with her own desire to be "average." Had I been accelerated through, or altogether out of, my general education courses, I can't say what kind of person and scholar I'd be now. Alternatively, if I'd been made to feel *less than* by virtue of having (many) fewer credits than more advantaged students, I don't know how or whether I would have finished college at all.

While overall nationwide trends in overall class- (and race-) based bifurcation of the collegiate population pre- and post-enrollment have been well documented (Mullen 2011; Stuber 2012; Stich 2014; Mettler 2014; Armstrong 2015; Lee 2016; Hamilton 2016), and while these complement broader theories of other underlying economic class structures and studies of the university as an economic system (Conley 2009; Cottom 2017;

Bowen and McPherson 2016; Servon 2018; Newfield 2008, 2016), much more work can be done in our field on the relationship between social class, pre-college credit, and general education curricula. Such work would recognize how, in this new campus economy, we have continued to obfuscate—in Rose's terms—the "abilities hidden by class and cultural barriers" (*Lives* xi) in the name of a streamlined curriculum that values the "effective, no-nonsense pedagogy we assume the past must have had" (7). In our haste to elide difference, we have changed the way we define *prepared,* and by extension, *literate*. The *boundary* of remediation has been socially and structurally extended beyond those in the vocational track at Our Lady of Mercy to a much wider range of students from various geographies and economies. These students without pre-college credit are told they must "catch up" to their peers. They are labeled remedial, even when their scholastic profiles are anything but, and even as general education was always meant to be a significant and core component of a liberal education. As Rose would say, these students are "already behind the economic and political eight ball" (127).

There's no easy road here, but I believe that WPAs can help turn back the tide toward a slower, more thoughtful way of valuing literacy acquisition and general education in our current economy, in part by continuing to research the class-based constraints and affordances that pre-determine students' pathways through the college experience. By recognizing the socioeconomic realities of how we move students through our curriculum, and what Mike Rose's immense body of work has taught us in this regard, WPAs can build and sustain inclusive writing programs that send the message that it's *OK*—even actually *good*—to be average.

Works Cited

Armstrong, Elizabeth A., and Laura T. Hamilton. *Paying for the Party: How College Maintains Inequality.* Harvard UP, 2015.

Bowen, Betsy and Kathryn Nantz. "What Is the Value of a GED?" *College English*, vol. 77, no. 1, 2014, pp. 32-54.

Bowen, William G. and Michael S. McPherson. *Lesson Plan: An Agenda for Change in American Higher Education.* Princeton UP, 2016.

Conley, Dalton. *Elsewhere, U.S.A.: How We Got from the Company Man, Family Dinners and the Affluent Society to the Home Office, BlackBerry Moms and Economic Anxiety.* Pantheon Books, 2009.

Cottom, Tressie McMillan. *Lower Ed: The Troubling Rise of For-Profit Colleges in the New Economy.* The New Press, 2017.

Hamilton, Laura T. *Parenting to a Degree: How Family Matters for College Women's Success.* U of Chicago P, 2016.

Hansen, Kristine and Christine R. Farris. *College Credit for Writing in High School: The "Taking Care" of Business*. National Council of Teachers of English, 2010.

Lee, Elizabeth M. *Class and Campus Life: Managing and Experiencing Inequality at an Elite College*. ILR Press, 2016.

Mettler, Suzanne. *Degrees of Inequality: How the Politics of Higher Education Sabotaged the American Dream*. Basic Books, 2014.

Mullen, Ann L. *Degrees of Inequality: Culture, Class, and Gender in Higher Education*. Johns Hopkins UP, 2011.

Newfield, Christopher. *Unmaking the Public University: The Forty Year Assault on the Middle Class*. Harvard UP, 2008.

—. The Great Mistake: How We Wrecked Public Universities and How We Can Fix Them. Johns Hopkins UP, 2016.

Rose, Mike. *Lives on the Boundary: A Moving Account of the Struggles and Achievements of America's Educationally Underprepared*. Penguin Books, 1990.

Servon, Lisa. *The Unbanking of America: How the New Middle Class Survives*. Mariner Books, 2018.

Stich, Amy. *Access to Inequality: Reconsidering Class, Knowledge, and Capital in Higher Education*. Lexington Books, 2012.

Kelly Ritter is professor and chair of the School of Literature, Media, and Communication at the Georgia Institute of Technology. Her scholarship focuses on archival histories of U.S. writing programs and pedagogies and the impact of cultural-historical conceptions of social class on literacy education. She is the author or editor of eight books, including the forthcoming *Beyond Fitting In: Rethinking First-Generation Writing and Literacy Education* (MLA, 2023). From 2012 to 2017, she served as editor of *College English*.

"Becoming fully and richly literate": Teaching Antiracism to Bring More Lives from the Boundaries

Kathleen Turner Ledgerwood

This article examines Mike Rose's work in Lives on the Boundary *as a foundational exploration of classist practices in writing. Rose calls for a rich literacy is a precursor to today's calls to expand literacy. A critical language approach helps pave a path for composition to incorporate antiracist practices*

In *Lives on the Boundary*, Mike Rose called for writing teachers, especially developmental English teachers, to not compare our work with medical diagnoses and fixes, to move away from teaching grammar and correctness through simple exercises, and to instead replace this by enriching our classrooms with the enjoyment of writing and languaging. As Rose talked about what he witnessed in developmental classes, he wrote, "It teaches them that the most important thing about writing–the very essence of writing–is grammatical correctness, not the communication of something meaningful, or the generative struggle with ideas . . . not even word play" (211). Rose called for us then to help students consider language in their "schools, jobs, and neighborhoods" (211). At the time, Rose was writing about developmental English classes and the students and curriculum most common there. His call to help students use their own everyday language really echoes the sentiment in the 1974 NCTE statement of "Student's Rights to Their Own Language." Rose called us again to affirm the process of students' languaging and to think about how we communicate meaningful ideas through writing.

As a graduate student and teaching assistant from a working-class background in the early 2000s, I read *Lives on the Boundary* as part of my teacher training class, and it resonated with me. When Mike Rose passed away, I thought back to how I identified with Rose while reading this book, thinking about class and society and helping students develop a love of language. I'm a queer, disabled, working-class assistant professor of English who is the writing program administrator at an open-access, historically Black university in the midwest. In my interactions with my students who fear failure, who have been traditionally underserved, and who many would call "underprepared," I grapple daily with thinking through how best to serve our students at an HBCU, where the majority of the students are black and from a lower socio-economic background. I believe that if we take Mike Rose's work with developmental English a step further and consider the role of race as well as socio-economic class in our writing classes, then we find ourselves enmeshed in the discussions of antiracist pedagogy. Composition professionals must consider our complicity in racist systems because we cannot ignore the ways in which racism and classism are enmeshed within our cultural ideologies of what constitutes "academic writing."

Rose's work calls us to think about our teaching. It begins discussions focused on our grading, and the ways in which we privilege some students through teaching a standardized English that focuses on a White Mainstream English, to the exclusion of the plurality of language, all for a monolingual focus on "correctness." Indeed, the rhetoric surrounding standardized language is a moralistic rhetoric that privileges some students while openly attacking other registers and languages. If we truly celebrate Rose's call for us to teach the richness of language, word play, and the communication of ideas above the idea of correctness, then we see that we must open our heuristics of grading and evaluation for a variety of Englishes. In Asao B. Inoue's 2019 Chair's address at CCCC, he asked us to move forward in the profession by moving past the perpetuation of White language supremacy and the teaching, assessing, giving feedback, and grading based on one, standardized English. Inoue told us that to maintain one standard of English is to "maintain White supremacy" (353). While many composition scholars, teachers, and activists embrace this call and seek to make systemic changes in order to not further the oppression of our students, many more argue that language does not define a person or a culture, or they argue that we cannot move beyond one standardized English. But as Toni Morrison explains, "It's terrible to think that a child with five different tenses comes to school to be faced with those books that are less than his own language. And then to be told things about his language, which is him, that are sometimes permanently damaging . . . This is a really cruel fallout of racism . . . " (qtd. in Lippi-Green 145). It is long overdue for us to listen to writers who call for us to open our practices and systems to translingual, plurilingual, accessible and socially just systems of teaching, evaluation, and grading in our classrooms.

Not only does stripping away someone's language perpetuate racism, but I believe that to continue to teach one monolithic English oppresses all of our students, in part because as Mike Rose was telling us in 1989, to focus on "correctness" also "fosters attitudes and beliefs about written language that, more than anything, *keep* students from becoming fully and richly literate" (211). Teaching a single standard of correctness to our students keeps them from being fully and richly literate; it further oppresses our students of color, and it perpetuates a White linguistic supremacy over other cultural linguistic practices. We must continue to work to bring in our colleagues and students who live marginalized or on boundaries. It's time to complete a calling in on our own curriculum and practices to find a way to break down boundaries in language education.

The logical progression from Mike Rose's call to help our students become "fully and richly literate" means that composition teachers should embrace teaching critical language awareness (CLA) in our writing classes. Sanchez and Paulson claim a better approach than remedial/basic skills is "one in which students learn not only how to read and write academic texts, but also how to examine critically the discourse that makes up their world(s)" (165). This is the same argument Rose makes about teaching students to think about language contexts and to think about what it might mean to change writing within a society with systemic racism and classism. Alim says the goal of CLA approaches is for "students [to] become conscious of their communicative behavior and the ways by which they can transform the conditions under which they live" (28). In order to change the racist, anti-black systems in education, we must begin to change the ways in which we teach about language and writing in our composition classes and our teacher education classes. We need to create the kind of Critical Race English Education (CREE) that Lamar L. Johnson began calling for in 2018, and we need to live up to the revolutionary hope for changing our educational systems in "This Ain't Another Statement! This is a DEMAND for Black Linguistic Justice!" from July of 2022. If we want to move forward, we must embrace teaching critical language awareness and open our practices to create fully and richly literate classrooms that invite all students to use their linguistic currency in our curriculums and to honor the tender that has been bought with so much cultural devastation and prejudice. I'm not going to pretend to know all the answers to begin this change, but I feel we move the work of Mike Rose forward by focusing on fully literate communities, when we open our classrooms up for students to use their own languages and change our teaching to begin to explore the rich literacies around us and interrogate the racist and unjust systems we perpetuate in our classes.

Works Cited

Alim, H. Samy. "Critical Language Awareness in the United States: Revisiting Issues and Revising Pedagogies in a Resegregated Society." *Educational Researcher*, vol. 34, no. 7, Oct. 2005, pp. 24–31, doi:10.3102/0013189X034007024.

Inoue, Asos B. "2019 CCCC Chair's Address: How Do We Language So People Stop Killing Each Other, Or What Do We Do About White Language Supremacy?" *College Composition and Communication*, vol. 71, no. 2, 2019, pp. 352-369.

Johnson, Lamar L. "Where Do We Go from Here? Toward a Critical Race English Education" *Research in the Teaching of English*, vol. 53, no. 2, November 2018, pp. 102-124.

Lippi-Green, Rosina. *English with and Accent: Language, Ideology, and Discrimination in the United States 2nd Edition.* New York: Routledge, 2012.

Rose, Mike. *Lives on the Boundary: The Struggles and Achievements of America's Underprepared.* New York: The Free Press, 1989.

Sanchez, Deborah M. and Eric J. Paulson. "Critical Language Awareness and Learners in College Transitional English" *Teaching English in the Two-Year College*, vol. 36, no.2, Dec 2008, pp. 164-176.

Kathleen Turner Ledgerwood is assistant professor of English and writing area coordinator at Lincoln University in Missouri. As a teacher-scholar-activist, she is very interested in equity-based, antiracist, and decolonizing teaching practices. This interest has led to research in how students deal with affect in regards to writing feedback and revision. In her spare time, you'll also find her studying and writing about popular media, especially film and television.

Mike Rose, the Rust Belt, and Me

Marjorie Stewart

A chance meeting with Mike Rose gave the author of this essay a chance to revisit his work to better understand her own. This serendipitous encounter focused on the love of story, on a mutual passion for helping underprepared students, and shared rust belt backgrounds. The layers of interconnecting narratives led to a lively conversation about what those commonalities meant to them as teachers. The essay offers serious reflection on the work of reading, writing, and teaching, and the importance of honoring those who have guided us through those activities.

I was in St. Louis Lambert International airport and heading home from CCCCs when my phone rang. It was my conference roommate telling me that I had left my keys at the hotel. After an initial moment of panic and a few false starts, we arrived at a plan: she would put the keys in a cab and send them my way. All I had to do was wait.

I am not a patient person. As I waited, I paced. As I paced, I noticed a familiar face at a gate near mine. It was Mike Rose. I was starstruck. Just days before I had hung onto every word of his exemplar acceptance speech. Needing something to do with my nervous energy, I scraped up the courage to approach him. He was open and friendly. "Call me Mike," he said immediately. I told him my story to justify my twitchiness; he sympathized and followed the unfolding tale of the keys and the forthcoming cabbie with interest.

We talked about our Pennsylvania rust belt backgrounds. I had moved earlier that year to rural West Virginia from Pittsburgh; he was familiar with the area, as he was a native of Altoona. He seemed to have a special fondness for Pittsburgh, and I told him of my only Altoona experience – riding a train around the Horseshoe Curve when I was about ten years old. We shared how we both missed close families, close neighborhoods, and the sense of community from our hometowns. We talked about places like Detroit, Cleveland, and the rest of the rust. I told him how the West Virginia coal industry was going the way steel went in Pittsburgh – clinging to false hope, promising a comeback that could never be. He understood.

That day in the airport I told Mike how my students were almost universally appalled at that attitude in "I Just Wanna Be Average" yet didn't recognize it in themselves. We talked about the importance of that story, of all stories, in connecting with students in the classroom. I shared the stories of my students (largely underprepared, first generation, and low income) and the emotional burdens and revelations they brought to the classroom. He talked about teaching and writing stories. The airport concourse faded into the background as narrative theory came alive.

I had discovered Rose's work my first year of teaching and followed him religiously thereafter. I taught at a college where several first-year writing professors used his work and some even used the entirety of *Lives on the Boundary*. I had been skeptical at first – did students want to read about how the educational system had failed them?

I had never set foot in a composition classroom until I was teaching in one. I had placed out of composition as an undergraduate and had not taught during my Masters' program. Fortunately, the writing program administrator invited me to team teach one of her sections with her, so I saw immediately how students related to Rose and his stories. That experience began my emphasis on narrative in the reading and the writing that I continue to assign. I use "Blue Collar Brilliance" in our English 102 class, which focuses on research writing. My students all know people, often family members, with blue collar jobs and already have great respect for them. The essay helps them identify and articulate what they had already known: there is a specialized kind of intelligence behind all work, whether it is respected in our culture or not.

I wish I could remember all the stories Mike told me that day in the airport – stories that flashed both back and forwards from those we knew and loved. What I remember is his charm, his smile and quick laugh, and his grace in spending time with a nervous fangirl worrying about her keys. He was tired – he said so and it showed. He was looking forward to going home and unwinding – "Conferences," he said, "were becoming exhausting."

As the conversation lapsed into silence, my phone rang. The cabbie was at the airport with my keys. All I had to do was get out and back in through security, and then it would be time to board my plane. He wished me luck again and said how he had enjoyed the conversation. I waved a quick goodbye over my shoulder. Glancing back, I saw him sink back into his seat, watching me dash off.

I tell the story of my meeting with Mike Rose when I introduce his work to students. My students read and workshopped this essay in class. They read "Blue Collar Brilliance" and "I Just Wanna Be Average" at the same time, which, like all his stories, meant more to me after that interlude in St. Louis and now they mean even more after his death. Mike Rose was my first scholar hero and the only one whom I ever met. Even though that was our only in person encounter, I miss you, Mike.

Marjorie Stewart is professor of English at Glenville State University. Before Dr. Stewart arrived at Glenville, she taught composition and directed the writers' center at the Art Institute of Pittsburgh. At GSU, she teaches first-year writing, concentrating on corequisite courses for students who are underprepared for college English. She also teaches journalism and creative nonfiction and sponsors the student newspaper, *The Phoenix*.

The Reading Labs: Pedagogical History and Humane Design

Luis E. Poza and Manuel Luis Espinoza

This brief essay describes Reading Labs, a pedagogical intervention implemented to support novice social science students with reading complex primary legal documents and composing analytic summaries and other collegiate writing. In this overview, the authors highlight the social nature of learning: how meanings were negotiated among participants deciphering laws and court opinions, how questions and peer feedback helped sharpen arguments and voice in students' written work. In so doing, the authors evoke Mike Rose's own work in writing programs across levels, relying on small, intimate groupings of students, serious regard given to their intellectual efforts including errors, and a pedagogy marked by encouragement and gentle questioning.

Vilma, a Mexican-American young woman and first-gen college student in a pre-service teacher pathway, reads aloud from the excerpted opinion of *McLaurin v. Oklahoma State Regents* (1950). Her peers, Mackenzie -- a white, female, first-gen college student from a rural stretch of the state, and Julius, a male Marine veteran identifying as mixed race (white and Filipino), follow along. The three have skimmed the opinion independently, and are joining this *Reading Lab* to more deeply engage with the text and clarify questions from their first reading.

> Appellant's case represents, perhaps, the epitome of that need, for he is attempting to obtain an advanced degree in education, to become, by definition, a leader and trainer of others. Those who will come under his guidance and influence must be directly affected by the education he receives. Their own education and development will necessarily suffer to the extent that his training is unequal to that of his classmates. State-imposed restrictions which produce such inequalities cannot be sustained[...] (*McLaurin* 641)

In ensuing discussions across Reading Labs, Vilma, Mackenzie, and Julius connect this reading to previous conversations about the 14th Amendment, which underlies this and other desegregation rulings. They debate the distinctions between *privileges* and *immunities* in legal discourse. In probing the intent and material reality of the term *equality* across texts, they interweave their own experiences–with sexism, under-resourced high schools, leaving behind homogenous hometowns to study in diverse urban campuses—and come to embody "the real stuff of belonging to an academic community" with "a richer, more transactive model of classroom discourse" (Hull & Rose 297). Their subsequent writing attests to "dynamic involvement in generating and questioning knowledge" and "a complete, active, struggling engagement with the facts and principles of a discipline, an encounter with the discipline's texts and the incorporation of them into one's own work, the framing of one's knowledge within the myriad conventions that help define a discipline" (Rose 359). With Manuel, the designer and primary instructor of the course, and Luis, a novice professor apprenticing to assume its instruction, sitting at the table but only interjecting sporadically with probing questions, the students demonstrate their ingenuity and deepen their analytic capacities by teasing apart complex legal writing and making connections to their future teaching.

But for these Reading Labs modeled after the writing and teaching of Mike Rose, this writing-intensive course examining human dignity and the educational process through landmark legal texts might overwhelm students like Vilma, Mackenzie, and Julius. Vilma herself expressed as much when she recalled the first week's assignments, "If those were the type of readings that we were going to get, I was not going to be able to complete the class with a good grade." She credited the Reading Labs with her success, "because they helped me understand, and also by having other people in here like [Julius] and [Mackenzie] and all them. It made me understand different perspectives…other points of view, what they caught and I didn't catch."

About one month after this Reading Lab session, the students were to submit their culminating writing assignment: their pedagogical song, an intertextual essay braiding together their own philosophy of teaching with the primary documents encountered throughout the course. Though an individual assignment, the Reading Labs afforded opportunities for collaboration and experimentation among students crafting their essays. In the mold of Mike Rose's exhortations for writing instruction, assignments were cumulative, such that analytic summaries of individual cases built up to this ultimate synthesis between the legal, historical, and personal aspects of schooling in US society and students' lives. In-class writing and discussion of writing were plentiful thanks to the Reading Labs, allowing students to attempt phrasings and passages in their work they might not undertake independently and to seek feedback from each other and from the two professors in attendance. Discussions of error were always in the context of students' writing, attending to their intended purpose and the textual influences they were summoning. Through such cycles of experimentation and feedback, students in the Reading Labs were able to appreciate "new ways of thinking about how language is used, what it does, and how an effect is achieved" (Rose 262).

It was through exchanges such as these that Vilma wavered and then decided to include *consejos* (advice) in Spanish passed down through her family alongside matching segments of landmark opinions, "Morals are spoken by *mi abuelo* [my grandfather] . . . '*Y sobre todo, nunca humilles a nadie*' [Above all, never humiliate anyone]…they shouldn't need to be stated by the Warren Court, 'To separate them from others of similar age and qualifications solely because of their race generates a feeling of inferiority as to their status in the community that may affect their hearts and minds" (*Brown* 494).

Indeed, despite her early self-doubt and insufficient high school preparation, Vilma's song masterfully accomplished the dual tasks of incisive legal, sociological, and personal analysis alongside complex writing for academic audiences. In its conclusion, the piece even mirrored the Court's reasoning in *McLaurin*,

> Without the occurrence of *Brown v. Board of Education*, I may not be able to pursue the career path that I am currently on. I would not be able to discuss *Plessy v. Ferguson* or *Roberts v. City of Boston* with my classmates of lighter skin complexity [sic]. I probably would not have been able to even enhance my education thus far. Yet, through the *Brown* rulings I am able to chase after my dream, which will give me the opportunity to provide my students with the proper tools to create who they will become.

Vilma's writing, emerging from her Reading Labs conversations, poignantly inserts her within the narrative of US history as a beneficiary of progress to date and an agent of changes still to come.

Though Vilma and others like her never studied with Mike Rose, they can be thought of as the "downstream" beneficiaries of his thinking, instruction, and intellectual generosity. With respect to the adaptive design of an educational environment, the Reading Labs "rhyme" with Rose's graduate writing courses—the intimacy of small numbers with all participants learning in some way, the serious attention paid to the thinking of students grappling with difficult texts, the encouragement communicated via a light pedagogical touch, and the possibility, often actualized, of young people walking away from an intellectual encounter more expert than when they arrived.

Works Cited

Hull, Glynda, and Mike Rose. "This Wooden Shack Place: The Logic of an Unconventional Reading." *College Composition and Communication* vol 41, no. 3, 1990, pp. 287–298.

Rose, Mike. "The Language of Exclusion: Writing Instruction at the University." *College English* vol. 47, no. 4, 1985, pp. 341–359.

Rose, Mike. "Rereading *Lives on the Boundary.*" *Traditions of Eloquence: The Jesuits and Modern Rhetorical Studies*, Fordham University Press, 2016, p. 261–263.

United States, Supreme Court. *Brown v. Board of Education.* vol. 347 17 May 1954. pp. 483, 74 S. Ct. 686, 98 L. Ed. 873.

United States, Supreme Court. *McLaurin v. Oklahoma State Regents for Higher Ed.*, vol. 339 (1950) 637, 70 S. Ct. 851, 94 L. Ed. 1149.

Luis E. Poza (https://orcid.org/0000-0002-6775-8719) is associate professor of teacher education in the Connie L. Lurie College of Education at San José State University. He teaches about multicultural education, bilingual education, and the roles of language and education in human rights frameworks. His research examines how ideologies of language, race, class, and nation are embedded and enacted in educational policy and practice for bilingual learners.

Manuel Luis Espinoza is associate professor at the University of Colorado at Denver in the School of Education and Human Development, where he works on issues of learning and civil rights. He is a child of desegregation (*Keyes v. Denver School District No. 1*, 1973) and a Chicano ethnographer and philosopher of education working in the scholarly tradition that emerged during the twentieth-century struggle against racism in the United States.

"Just as I have a mind": Mike Rose and the Intelligence of Ordinary People

John Trimbur

This essay looks at the social democratic roots of Mike Rose's belief in the intelligence of ordinary people and the educability of poor and working-class kids currently bypassed by the education system. His later work, especially The Mind at Work, *challenges the narrowing effects of the division of mental and manual labor in class society, imagining instead the inventive interplay of mind, heart, and hand.*

Mike Rose was a social democrat in the finest lower-case, non-doctrinaire sense of the term. He was an educational reformer, like Horace Mann and John Dewey, who championed the public education of an active citizenry. Like Walt Whitman, Mike believed in the infinite potential of the common people, the democratic vistas and practical intelligence of the popular classes. And like the English arts-and-crafts socialist William Morris, Mike was a visionary who imagined the inventive interplay of mind, heart, and hand; thought and action; aesthetics and labor.

What animated Mike was the injustice of a class society that excludes ordinary men and women from elite forms of knowledge, limits their participation in public life, and squanders their latent abilities and talents. His mission, accordingly, was to figure out how the monopoly of epistemic power that benefits the few could be redistributed to the many: to the underclass of partially educated students he encountered in Voc. Ed. classes in high school, the Vietnam vets he tutored, and the underprepared kids he taught in the Equal Opportunity Program at UCLA.

***

Mike grew up in the ethnic class culture of southern European migrants who settled in the industrial centers of the east and midwest, families where no one went to college and many didn't finish high school, taking factory jobs instead. In *Lives on the Boundary*, Mike has a keen awareness of his worried parents, poised between the instability of working-class jobs and the perils of small-proprietor business operations, like the Spaghetti House restaurant his father ran for a few years in Altoona, Pennsylvania, until he had to close it when the Pennsylvania Railroad shut down and the local economy in Altoona collapsed. The family moved to Los Angeles, and Mike's mother supported them working as a waitress.

Mike lived the rest of his life in Los Angeles. In the late 1950s, when he was in high school, this meant the allure of beatniks, non-conformist high school English teachers, and the various bohemian subcultures of Southern California that withheld consent in the Eisenhower era to the mainstream view of American life on *Father Knows Best* and *Ozzie & Harriet*–harbingers of the counterculture and New Left about to emerge in the 1960s. Like the disaffected youth of his time, he wrote poetry, watched films at L.A.'s small art-house cinemas, and listened to Black music. He came of age, that is, in an anti-union city of celluloid dreams, on the verge of startling political and cultural change.

***

Mike registers these changes in *Lives on the Boundary*, when he takes readers on a walk through Campbell Hall at UCLA sometime in the mid-1970s, when "the walls were covered with posters, flyers, and articles clipped from the newspaper . . . calls for legal defense funds and vigils for justice. There was news about military atrocities in Chile, CIA murders in Africa, the uprooting of the American Indian" (169). The anti-Vietnam War movement, Black power, and Third World politics had upended the old order on college campuses, politicizing a generation and raising new questions about access to college and the educability of poor and working-class students–Black and white, Latinx, Asian American, and Indigenous–formerly excluded by selective admissions. Open admissions was just starting at the CUNY colleges, the result of demonstrations and lobbying by a loose coalition of the Black and Puerto Rican Student Community at City College, the New York City Central Labor Council, and assorted radicals and reformers.

Mike comes into view in U.S. college composition at a moment intent on democratizing higher education, in the era of open admissions, the founding of Equal Opportunity Programs, and the refashioning of old-school remedial "bonehead" English courses into basic writing. Like his counterparts on the East Coast at CUNY–who included not only notable compositionists such as Mina Shaughnessy and John Brereton but also the postcolonial critic Aijaz Ahmad (who briefly directed the SEEK program at City College) and writers and poets like June Jordan, Toni Cade Bambara, and Adrienne Rich–Mike was seeking a richer use of language, a more open form of education, and an understanding of how the complex logics of error might unlock students' ways of knowing.

***

For Mike, the keyword was intelligence, and the educational imperative was to redefine it–to delink it from the measurement of standardized testing with its predictable white, middle-class norms and to see it instead as a form of intellectual work that students from underserved educational backgrounds apply to reading and writing. As Mike shows over and over in *Lives on the Boundary* and in articles like "'This Wooden Shack Place': The Logic of an Unconventional Reading," with Glynda Hull, what may appear on the surface to be poor student performances, pathologized by the dominant medical vocabulary of remediation, can, in the realm of pedagogical practice, be unpacked and elaborated as the grounds of learning rather than corrected as an absence of knowledge.

This, at any rate, is how composition and writing studies have conventionally pictured Mike's legacy–how he, along with Mina Shaughnessy, David Bartholomae, Patricia Bizzell, and assorted others, changed the way we read student writing, setting out the theoretical/pedagogical groundwork not just for basic writing but, more widely, for the emergent field of a modern composition and its resistance to what Mike called the "cognitive reductionism" and "language of exclusion" in the American university (see "Narrowing the Mind and Page" and "The Language of Exclusion at the University"). Often left out of this standard portrait, however, is Mike's later work, after he moved from the undergraduate writing program to the School of Education at UCLA.

The Mind at Work: Valuing the Intelligence of the American Worker, for example, considerably complicates our understanding of Mike's lifework, operating on non-academic terrain, investigating everyday working-class jobs and the practical intelligence of waitresses, carpenters, electricians, and hair stylists. *The Mind at Work*, as Mike makes clear, is meant to repay his debt to earlier immigrant generations of working-class men and women by recognizing—and honoring—the kinds of intelligence enacted through manual labor. But it is also meant to call into question the imputed hierarchy of blue-collar and white-collar work itself, to challenge the ideological underpinnings of the class distinctions between mental and manual labor, academic knowledge and vocational education.

The official mission (if not always the reality) of American higher education, of course, has been to lift working-class kids into middle-class jobs, and it may not be self-evident at first glance what writing studies and mainstream college composition programs might make of Mike's later work on the dignity and complexity of labor, in particular his interest in integrating vocational and academic education. Part of the difficulty comes from the longstanding conceptual impasse in composition between "pragmatic" approaches, on one hand, that teach for real-world careers and/or academic success and "critical" pedagogies, on the other, that aspire to make students more active and aware as citizens and political agents.[1] As Min-Zhan Lu and Bruce Horner have suggested, however, it is altogether thinkable to dissolve the pragmatic/critical binary and imagine a writing course that investigates the meanings of such keywords as "careers," "mobility," and "skills" in the unsettled division of labor that has emerged with the shift from the older Fordist economy, with its lifetime careers of "company men" and relatively stable union jobs, to the mobility of deterritorialized portfolio men and women and the precariousness of flexible labor in the era of "fast capitalism."

***

I am drawn to such a vision of "critical vocationalism" and the possibilities it raises, in single writing classrooms, certainly, but also, especially, in non-corporate professional writing majors, where students can explore over time the distribution, uses, constraints, and untapped potentialities of the available means of communication–where the acquisition of vocational skills and academic critique are in constant interaction. To be sure, I realize that in the final analysis such initiatives, for all their merits and attractions, are inescapably part of the same old class reproduction and its hierarchies of mental and manual labor. But this is precisely why I think Mike's *The Mind at Work* is important–because it offers not so much a programmatic blueprint as an orientation toward how we think about intelligence, the class divisions between blue-collar and white-collar labor, and the intertwined realities of work and school.

Rattling through the back of my mind are Karl Marx's words about how the prevailing division of labor restricts humans to an "exclusive sphere of activity, which is forced on them and from which they cannot escape." What Marx imagined instead was the negation of the prevailing division of labor, to replace its mind/body, mental/manual dichotomies with self-determining multi-dimensional individuals who "hunt in the morning, fish in the afternoon, raise cattle in the evening, criticize, just as a I have a mind, without ever becoming a hunter, fisherman, herdsman, or critic" (53).

Just as I have a mind: these words linger, marking the radical affirmation in Mike's work of the intelligence of ordinary people against the narrowing effects of schooling and the stifling divisions of mental and manual labor. This is what enabled Mike to imagine, at least in broad outline, an educational future that circumvents the classic liberal formula of equalizing opportunity (and thereby legitimizing the inevitably unequal results).

Mike's investigations of intelligence at school and work led him rather to sense what you might call the "not-yet" that is lurking unrealized in the contradictory realities of class society, the latent possibilities of meaning-making and social-being that might help us anticipate how to expand the actual scope and capacities of the human personality, to make individuals fit for more generous and wide-ranging participation in a truly social democracy.

NOTE

1. The "pragmatic/critical" split can be dated, at least symbolically, to the 1999 appearance of Russel Durst's *Collision Course: Conflict, Negotiation, and Learning in College Composition* and the subsequent exchange between William Thelin ("Understanding Problems of Critical Pedagogy" and "Response to Russel Durst") and Durst ("Can We Be Critical of Critical Pedagogy?").

WORKS CITED

Durst, Russel. "Can We Be Critical of Critical Pedagogy?" *College Composition and Communication*, vol. 58, no. 1, 2006, pp. 110–114.
—. *Collision Course: Conflict, Negotiation, and Learning in College Composition.* NCTE, 1999.
Lu, Min-Zhan and Bruce Horner. "Composing in a Global-Local Context: Careers, Mobility, Skills." *College English*, vol. 72, no. 2, 2008, pp. 113–133.
Marx, Karl. *The German Ideology.* Edited with an introduction by C.J. Arthur. International Publishers, 1970.
Rose, Mike. *Lives on the Boundary.* Penguin, 1990.
—. The Language of Exclusion: Writing Instruction at the University." *College English*, vol. 47, no. 4, pp. 341–359.
—. *The Mind at Work: Valuing the Intelligence of the American Worker.* Penguin, 2004.
—. Narrowing the Mind and Page: Remedial Writers and Cognitive Reductionism." *College Composition and Communication*, vol. 39, no. 3, 1988, pp. 267–302.
—. and Glynda Hull. "'This Wooden Shack Place': The Logic of an Unconventional Reading." *College Composition and Communication*, vol. 41, no. 3, 1990, pp. 287–298.
Thelin, William. "Response to Russel Durst." *College Composition and Communication*, vol. 58, no. 1, 2006, pp. 114–118.
—. "Understanding Problems in Critical Classrooms." *College Composition and Communication*, vol. 57, no. 1, 2005, pp. 114–141

John Trimbur is emeritus professor ofrhetoric and writing studies at Emerson College. His most recent book is *Grassroots Literacy and the Written Record: A Textual History of Asbestos Activism in South Africa* (Multilingual Matters, 2020).

Mike Rose's Two-Year College Advocacy

Darin L. Jensen and Cheryl Hogue Smith

As community college faculty, the authors know that Mike Rose was a champion of our institutions. The dialogue here reflects both his personal influence on the authors as literacy workers and on two-year college English studies.

Darin: I was teaching in Omaha at Metro Community College in a program for high school dropouts when a colleague handed me *Lives on the Boundary*. I was struck by the first line: "This is a hopeful book about those who fail." The book explores language in human connection, literacy, and culture and focuses on those who have trouble reading and writing in schools and in the workplace. I had found someone who directly spoke to my work. His work has shaped my entire practice as a community college teacher and literacy professional.

Cheryl: I first read this in a graduate class at Cal State Bakersfield, where I was also teaching. So I didn't first read it through a community college lens. It's interesting that you thought he was talking to you, and I thought he was talking to me.

Darin: He was talking to us.

Cheryl: Right, right.

Darin: In the first chapter of *Lives on the Boundary*, Rose turns our understanding of literacy history on its head: others use statistics to demonstrate educational decay, but Mike saw our literacy crisis through the perspective provided by another set of numbers, and he talks about how literacy rates have risen the last 60-70 years. His counter-argument pushes against manufactured literacy crises that arise cyclically as well as the testing and standardization culture which have emerged from those moral panics. Mike's work demonstrates that these moments have always been more about who we're letting in and what kinds of literacy we privilege.

Cheryl: That dovetails with *Back to School*: "I want to return to those dreary statistics about student success. . . . Some of us are also concerned that these aggregate rates of completion degrees and rates of transfer don't reflect the multiple reasons why people go to community college and why they leave" (13). He describes two students who left community college–one for the Navy, "where he could continue his education," and one after she had earned enough credits "to get a better job in her company"–students who many would claim "would be recorded as dropouts, a failure both for them and their college" (13).

Darin: That echoes back to *Lives on the Boundary*: we keep moving the goalposts for literacy rather than having an authentic conversation about what literacy is.

Cheryl: Yes. Mike kept saying we cannot use the same evaluative processes for two- and four-year colleges because students who enter two-year colleges don't necessarily have the same goals as those who enter a four-year.

Darin: That's important. We always talk about completion rate as in "how many years." The American Association of Community Colleges (AACC) has developed another way of quantifying success (AACC). But, Mike is talking about that at least a decade before anybody else. He saw that problem. You earlier said he was "prescient"; he saw how we were going to paint community colleges as not being successful, when what we were really looking at was a different measure of success. We seem trapped in a language of schooling that stresses economics, accountability, and compliance. Not only did Mike understand the way we're called "failures" but how the response has been to narrow everything down to these pathways that essentially say, "This is what school is; we're gonna make you a widget."

Cheryl: His body of work speaks to what others consider failure and what they do with it. Those who have never taught at community college, and I would include in that number some administrators who work at community colleges, don't understand that students' failures aren't necessarily failures. Thus, they indiscriminately implement programs, trying to fit us all into a box of success *they* have defined. That community colleges are constantly "redesigned" by people who don't understand them is absurd. In their eyes, we're failures; in our eyes, we know we're not. Do we fail some students? Of course, but that doesn't mean we're failures.

Darin: Mike got community college in ways that other scholars, especially scholars at four-year universities, don't. Part of that is, I think, because he was a first-generation kid who grew up poor, and his mom was a waitress, and his dad was sick. He used personal experience as a lens through which to understand the human consequences of what we do as two-year college literacy workers, and it's what makes him important. Large-scale reforms from places like Lumina or the Gates Foundation apply business logics of efficiency to something that is human and messy. Lives aren't just on the boundary; lives are also complicated. In *The Mind at Work*, Mike's showing us how to value other kinds of intelligences. Think of a tile worker who can look at a room and say, "This is how much tile we need, and this is how it should be cut." That has levels of intelligence and skill many of us don't have, yet some denigrate it.

Cheryl: He also noticed the corporatization of community colleges. Just look at the administrative bloat and how some Presidents are calling students "customers."

Darin: "Customer" comes from "custom house"; it means "to buy a credential." And that's not what "student" means. And it's a fundamental misunderstanding of what education is. More than that, it's a fundamental conflict about what education is about: admin are making it about something people can buy, and I want it to be something that people have a right to earn.

Cheryl: Right. It's a deliberate attempt to distort. It's deliberate, absolutely deliberate. Mike was always trying to temper what people were doing *to* community colleges. That's not to say we don't have room for improvement; we do, and Mike was always the first to say so.

Darin: In *Why School?* Mike says, "If we in some way constrict the full range of everyday cognition, then we will develop limited educational programs and fail to make fresh and meaningful instructional connections among disparate kinds of skills and knowledge" (96-97). That kind of functionalist narrow model takes away so much choice that it takes away from possibility.

Cheryl: With Mike gone, we collectively have to be that loud voice that explains what a community college *really is* versus what everyone else thinks it *should be*. Otherwise, we're going to become the automatons they want us to be.

Darin: Yes. It's *our* responsibility now; it's literacy workers in two-year college writing studies and writing programs that have that work in front of them. Most importantly, we must emphasize that one-size-fits-all reforms will not work.

Cheryl: Very true. Just look at, say, the "elimination" of developmental education and placement reform.

Darin: Yes, as we address the needs of two-year college literacy work, we must focus on placement. We know placement systems are embedded in local ecosystems which are inequitable. This doesn't mean that placement systems are automatically applied unfairly or are automatically inaccurate or that they are automatically fairly applied with an understanding of the best practices of placement and with a conscious effort to address and ameliorate (elimination may not be possible) the inequities of placement.

Cheryl: And that gets to the elimination of developmental education, which isn't really an elimination as much as it is a redistribution. Unless a program is integrating reading and writing instructions in all levels of composition, students will not receive the attention to reading that they need. We're seeing it in first-year writing, where the needs of students have been blurred and the class becomes a mixture of prepared and those who need more support. First-year writing classes of today are reminiscent of dev-ed classes of yore. And it's because people who have no business making decisions are making decisions, and our classes are filled with multiple skill levels of students, which makes targeted instruction much more difficult and belies the very fabric of completion and persistence.

Darin: This work will require a deep revisioning of literacy studies as a transdisciplinary effort. Concomitant with that, we must be teacher-scholar-activists who engage in the front-facing work of advocating for our students and discipline before anyone else imagines it for us. Essentially, we are in a struggle to write the narrative of literacy studies for the 21st century two-year college. Our students' lives–and perhaps our democracy–depends upon it.

WORKS CITED

American Association of Community Colleges. "Data Points: Student Completion and Persistence." 28 Feb. 2018, https://www.aacc.nche.edu/2018/02/28/data-points-student-completion-persistence/
Rose, Mike. *Lives on the Boundary*. New York: Penguin Books, 1990.
—. *The Mind at Work: Valuing the Intelligence of the American Worker*. Penguin, 2005.
—. *Why School?: Reclaiming Education for All of Us*. The New Press, 2014.
Rose, Mike, and Michael Anthony Rose. *Back to School: Why Everyone Deserves a Second Chance at Education*. The New Press, 2012.

Darin L. Jensen is assistant professor in the English, linguistics, and writing studies department at Salt Lake Community College He edits *Teaching English in the Two-Year College (TETYC)* and the Teacher-Scholar-Activist blog.

Cheryl Hogue Smith is professor of English at Kingsborough Community College of the City University of New York. She is the Immediate Past Chair of the Two-Year College English Association (TYCA).

"I Didn't Know How Else to Get It Right": *Lives on the Boundary* as an Invitation to Public Intellectualism

Ryan Skinnell

For nearly four decades, Mike Rose was one of the most successful public intellectuals in rhetoric and composition, and he routinely encouraged his colleagues to engage more intentionally with non-academic audiences. Lives on the Boundary *continues to provide a valuable model for considering how and why.*

In February 2019, the *Chronicle of Higher Education* published an article that rehearsed an old canard about the growing distance between academics and people. According to Michael C. Desch, professor of international relations at the University of Notre Dame, the problem is that "scholars increasingly privilege rigor over relevance," and therefore alienate themselves. Desch implies a lost golden age when academics were effectively and efficiently public and mourns its loss. But the supposed gap between academics and non-academics is at best a mischaracterization gleaned from cherry-picked examples. In fact, although academics cannot *not* be public to some degree, we are nevertheless still learning to be public intellectually. Fortunately, nearly 35 years after it was published, Mike Rose's *Lives on the Boundary* remains a guiding light in that regard.

There are two things in particular that *Lives on the Boundary* calls us to recognize and grapple with. The first is about the nature of public intellectual work itself. At the end of his preface, Rose notes that *Lives on the Boundary* is "both vignette and commentary, reflection and analysis" (xii). By way of explanation for this apparently strange hybrid genre, he writes, "I didn't know how else to get it right." As promised, Rose goes on to write a book that is highly readable, markedly academic, personally anecdotal, thoroughly researched, and occasionally downright poetic. It is both public and intellectual.

Rose's passage about "getting it right" is significantly more complex than it appears on the page, and as such is a skillful performance of the argument itself. His implicit argument is this: public intellectualism is not a message from one sphere to another—from academic to public or vice versa. It is not one's concession to the other's values. Rather, it is a rendering of *public* and *intellectual* together. As Anna M. Young and Jennifer Mercieca put it in a 2021 article arguing for the value of public scholarship in academic journals, "Public scholarship is a kind of citizenship" that attempts "to address the multiple and devastating problems of our moment"

(382). It's not just about research; it's also about living better together in the world. In attempting to get public intellectualism right to the same end, Rose conjures a hybrid genre in which both public and intellectualism are necessary work because it sincerely values both.

Rose makes the point even more clearly in "Writing for the Public." In that essay, he reflects on writing *Lives on the Boundary* for public audiences and on his efforts to teach writing for public audiences at UCLA. He writes of his teaching, "I encourage a kind of bilingualism, the continued development of facility with both scholarly writing and writing for non-specialists. But there is playback, as well, from the opinion piece and magazine article onto the writing students do for their disciplines" (289). This playback is what he performs in *Lives on the Boundary* and elsewhere.

Rose's nod to bilingualism is particularly illuminating. Bilingualism has been shown to have significant effects on cognition, on higher order thinking, on memory, and on focus. In other words, bilingualism isn't two languages existing side by side in a single human container. Bilingualism represents a functional, efficient hybridity of language use. The development of one language informs and is informed by development in other languages. They necessarily bleed into one another. Rose's rendering of the public and intellectual together exemplifies the same sort of mutually informing, hybrid process. This hybrid is what he performs in *Lives on the Boundary*, and it leads to the second point of consideration.

What distinguishes *Lives on the Boundary* from other calls to bridge the academic-public gap is the method by which the call is sounded. In his *Chronicle* essay, like so many authors who have issued similar calls, Desch works primarily in the medium of shame. His not-so-subtle message is that scholars have alienated themselves and need to shape up or face dire consequences. Rose, characteristically, works in a different medium—the medium of invitation.

Lives on the Boundary is an invitation to writing teachers to inhabit the hybrid genre of public and intellectual, which simultaneously reminds us how hard learning (and re-learning) to write is. Reflecting on his own writing for public audiences, Rose summarizes his beliefs about the importance of public intellectualism and its challenges. "The fostering of a hybrid professional identity—the life lived both in specialization and in the public sphere—is something I think we as a society need to nurture. The more opinion is grounded on rich experience and deep study, the better the quality of our public discourse about the issues that matter to us" (289). Again, for Rose, the form of "getting it right" unites the public and the intellectual that we all embody. But he also calls us to acknowledge the lessons we teach our students: learning to write is hard, and it takes time, motivation, practice, persistence, investment, and support.

It is hard to overstate the importance of this lesson. As teachers of writing, we invite students to become writers and wait patiently for them to accept the invitation. This is the pedagogy of the open hand. We honor students' needs and resist their demands, and we nurture their development in myriad ways, and we do this all through the mundane instruments of writing assignments, drafts, peer review, feedback, revision, and so on. Rose urges us, kindly but insistently, to practice publicly what we preach pedagogically.

This message seems especially urgent in the current moment, in a time of rising international authoritarianism and pressing global crises, but as Rose's book should remind us, it was always urgent. "Getting it right" is a commitment to publics and intellectualism that exceeds our immediate crises, which is one reason why *Lives on the Boundary* continues to be prescient more than three decades after it was published.

In *Prophets, Gurus, and Pundits*, rhetorician Anna Young notes that a significant challenge of public intellectualism is that "today's intellectuals often view themselves as lone discoverers . . . and distant observers . . . rather than as participants in the sociopolitical conditions of the public sphere" (2). But Rose's model of "getting it right" suggests methods for re-engaging intellectuals and publics that are desirable, practical, and socially valuable. Rose neither brings the academy to the publics nor vice versa, but merges the two, with his own experiences as the conduit. In so doing, he provides an invitation and a model for how we can "attend to both our field and the public domain...and find something generative in considering the two together" that should resonate with writing teachers and administrators (*Lives* 291).

Notes

I initially developed the ideas in this essay for a presentation at CCCC to celebrate the 30th anniversary of *Lives on the Boundary*. Mike didn't attend, but he emailed me after the fact, asked to read my paper, and wrote me a long response. It was one of the thrills of my life. One thing that stood out especially was a postscript he put in one of his emails to me: "You'll get a kick out of this," he wrote. "I hate the term 'public intellectual.' I get the point it makes, for sure, but it just rubs me the wrong way, sounds so high faultin' and self-important. I can picture my Uncle Joe, rest his soul, rolling his eyes." I picture Mike doing the same, rest his soul.

Acknowledgments

My thanks, of course, go to the editors for organizing this special issue and for their helpful feedback. My thanks especially goes to Mike Rose, Jonathan Alexander, and David Wallace for their involvement in bringing these thoughts to life in the first place.

Works Cited

Desch, Michael C. "How Political Science Became Irrelevant." *Chronicle of Higher Education*, 17 Feb 2019.
Rose, Mike. *Lives on the Boundary*. Penguin. 2005.
Young, Anna M. *Prophets, Gurus, and Pundits: Rhetorical Styles and Public Engagement*. Southern Illinois UP. 2019.
Young, Anna M., and Jennifer Mercieca. "Putting the 'Public' in *Rhetoric & Public Affairs*." *Rhetoric & Public Affairs*, vol. 24, no. 1-2, Spring-Summer 2021, pp. 379-95.

Ryan Skinnell is an associate professor of rhetoric and writing and an assistant writing program administrator at San José State University. He has published six books, including *Faking the News: What Rhetoric Can Teach Us About Donald J. Trump* (2018) and *Rhetoric and Guns* (2022). He has also published more than 80 articles, book chapters, and op-eds for academic and non-academic audiences on topics ranging from demagoguery, fascist rhetoric, and contemporary political discourse to American education, bureaucracy, and faculty development. He is currently writing a book about Hitler's rhetoric, which he intends to publish with a trade press.

My Mike Rose: The Library, Mom, and Critical Reading in *Lives on the Boundary*

Alice S. Horning

This piece captures the author's personal experience with Mike Rose that occurred as a by-product of her finding, more or less by chance, and reading Lives on the Boundary, *a book that captures important features of academic critical literacy of students then and now. To honor his legacy, writing studies faculty and all others in higher education must work to develop students' ability to read, write, speak and listen effectively, efficiently and critically.*

I was in my local public library, browsing the New Books shelves, and saw the name Rose and the title *Lives on the Boundary* among the biographies. "Is that *my* Mike Rose?" I thought to myself. What is he doing here, in the public library, on the biography shelf? I took it home and, like everyone else, loved it. And raved about it every chance I got, including to my mother, who, at 86, was still living independently in Florida. Always an active reader, she went to her library and got it; she read it and loved it too. I had read Rose's other work earlier, and I think I had been an anonymous reviewer for his *CCC* article with Glynda Hull ("This Wooden Shack Place: The Logic of an Unconventional Reading") so I recognized the style. In *Lives*, which won more than one award as I recall, Mike tells his own story in a compelling way, but then uses his emotional grasp on the reader to make an equally compelling argument about the need for changes in our system of education and our treatment of students. His argument is still valid today. Subsequently, I saw Mike at a conference and told him this story. He asked me to write down my mother's address and sent her a signed copy. She was surprised and delighted. That's just the kind of guy Mike Rose was. While I wanted to tell this story, I also wanted to show that what Rose says in *Lives* specifically about critical reading still needs our attention more than thirty years later.

In his chapter "Entering the Conversation" where Rose describes his early college experiences developing skills in critical literacy, it is impossible not to get drawn into his story of visiting a kind of intellectual club that he was ill-equipped to join. With the help of his teachers at Loyola in Los Angeles, he made his way in, largely through developing an ability to read academic texts. His teachers offered guidance through questions that led to what we currently call "deep reading" (Sullivan et al.) and vocabulary development combined with a lot of support and encouragement (cf.

Rose 158). Rose makes clear his own problems then and those for students now. Recent research shows that students' reading issues are still very much with us (Baron; Culver and Hutchens; Wolf) and have far-reaching implications: college completion, workforce readiness, democratic participation, and social justice (Noble). I have pointed repeatedly to students' "don't, won't, can't" problems with reading: they have limited reading experience in all their lives before college; they resist substantive reading of all kinds, but especially textbooks and many kinds of nonfiction prose, despite reading and writing for hours on social media, and they really can't do the kind of close, deep, critical reading of extended texts on paper or online that is essential to their success in school, careers, and as citizens in a democracy.

Rose offers a focused definition of critical literacy that is urgently needed, now more than ever:

> . . . framing an argument or taking someone else's argument apart, systematically inspecting a document, an issue or an event, synthesizing different points of view, applying a theory to disparate phenomena and so on. . . . Ours is the first society in history to expect so many of its people to be able to perform these very sophisticated literacy activities. (188)

Again using his own story, he explains that even in his doctoral dissertation, instead of writing an analytical description of his methodology, he wrote the story of his project. His adviser accused him of writing *Travels with Charley* instead of a dispassionate account of his research (189). He does not say how he responded to this critique, but did, after all, get a degree. He goes on from this point to show that error and backtracking to more familiar strategies are indicators of progress and effort. All of us have students who can tell a story, summarize a chapter (maybe), or report an event, but we do not make sufficient use of evidence-based teaching of strategies that equip students to move ahead to read and think critically. Are graduate programs preparing faculty to offer such strategies in the classroom, and do we know what they are?

The first question is one I have answered elsewhere in one word, NO (Horning). A review of a national sample of graduate programs in writing studies shows very few courses in the teaching of postsecondary critical reading anywhere. The second question is more complicated, but new studies are emerging that show the kinds of approaches that make a difference in students' critical skills. For example, the Stanford History Education researchers have found that lateral reading significantly improves critical judgment of online materials (Wineburg et al.; Breakstone et al.). The well-known CRAAP acronym (Currency, Relevance, Authority, Accuracy, and Purpose) also has a research basis, but it requires teaching key skills to make sure students can evaluate for these criteria. Students must also have strategies to *do* the evaluation, like the afore-mentioned lateral reading, which entails going beyond looking at a website itself to move laterally to see comparable information, check facts, and investigate claims made. It's not enough, then, just to teach the lateral reading approach or the acronym; information literacy is also needed to understand where information comes from and how it is accessed (Head et al.).

This kind of fuller understanding the online landscape is essential because it reveals the "algorithms of oppression" (Noble) and other ways that our access to information is being controlled and curated, leading to what one technology journalist has called the "infocalypse," defined as "the increasingly dangerous and untrustworthy information ecosystem within which most humans now live" (Schick 10). Classroom-based, evidence-based approaches are presented in the CCCC Position Statement on the Role of Reading in College Writing Classrooms (https://cccc.ncte.org/cccc/the-role-of-reading). But while these focused strategies are definitely needed, to follow Rose's approach, faculty must attend closely to students as people with complex lives. It is his stories of working with individual students, attending to their personal needs as well as their intellectual and critical literacy development, that made everyone love this book.

As but one example of his teaching philosophy, Rose makes a particularly poignant case for what we would now call Intersectionality, telling the story of a boy named Harold Morton whom Rose worked with in his second year in the Teacher Corps program at USC. Harold was a fifth grader who had lots of challenges with reading and writing that appeared to have a basis in some physical or psychological problems. When Rose started to build a relationship with Harold, he began to do better in school. When he visited Harold's home, met his mother and learned that his father had abandoned the family and was in jail at the time, many of Harold's problems began to make sense (Rose 114-127). Despite a lot of testing, assorted diagnoses and ideas for how to work with him, Rose saw that "Harold was made stupid by his longing, and his folder full of tests could never reveal that" (127). And yet, Rose had seen that Harold was perfectly capable of doing schoolwork, just needing attention and support.

To help this youngster, Rose relied less on specific teaching techniques or approaches and more on time and attention (116-118). While fifth grade is a long way from our classrooms and programs, this story, along with Rose's own make clear the importance of seeing all of the factors that affect students' performance. In other examples with older students, like those in the veterans' program where Rose taught for a time, he used a more focused approach, moving the students, step-by-step, from summary to classification, to comparison and finally to analysis (143–146). He points out that this particular group of students had complicated lives and experiences but little contact with academic texts and ideas, so providing connections they could grasp was a key to developing their critical literacy abilities. His example of Willie (146–148), one of the veterans who had spent time in prison and read a great deal, makes clear how a lifetime of experiences in combination with careful teaching can, through a personal and human connection, open a door into literacy, an education and a different life outcome.

This concept of Intersectionality, as presented by UCLA and Columbia law professor Kimberlé Crenshaw, captures this point: critical reading is an essential and urgently-needed ability we should be teaching aggressively to all students, but it overlaps with and is affected by everything else going on in their lives. Rose makes clear that we must do this work in the context of students' lives as they are, especially in these times as our lives have been complicated by the pandemic and all its implications. Now, perhaps more than ever, his message is that faculty must really believe in students' ability to do the work as he saw with Harold, and give them both the substantive tools and the needed personal support. The analytical and evaluative skills can and should be taught, maybe with the help of those faculty librarians who have deep knowledge of information literacy. All faculty, but especially first-year writing faculty who teach almost all college students, have a specific responsibility to develop students' skills in critical reading for authority, accuracy, and for bias of all kinds.

The thing about *Lives* is that Rose pulls readers (including Mom and me) into the story of his own education and that of others in a way that is particularly appealing for anyone involved in education (like me) or who cares about students, teaching and learning (as my mother did, maybe because of me). But in his time and ours, he rightly shows how an education in critical literacy is urgently needed. As he says at the end of *Lives*, to reach this goal we will need many blessings: "A philosophy of language and literacy that affirms diverse sources of linguistic competence and deepens our understanding of the ways class and culture blind us to the richness of those sources" (238). Working to prepare faculty appropriately to focus on this goal and making it central in our programs and courses would surely do justice to his legacy.

Works Cited

Baron, Naomi. *How We Read Now: Strategic Choices for Print, Screen &Audio.* Oxford UP, 2021.

Breakstone, Joel, Mark Smith, Sam Wineburg, Amie Rapaport, Jill Carle, Marshall Garland, and Anna Saavedra. "Students' Civic Online Reasoning: A National

Portrait." *Educational Researcher*, vol. 50, no. 8, 2021, pp. 505–15, https://doi.org/10.3102/0013189X211017495.

Culver, Tiffany, and Scott Hutchens. "Toss the Text? An Investigation of Student and Faculty Perspectives on Textbook Reading." *Journal of College Reading and Learning*, vol. 51, no. 2, 2021, pp. 81–94. DOI: 10.1080/10790195.2020.1734884

Crenshaw, Kimberle W. *On Intersectionality: Essential Writings*. Free Press, 2022.

Head, Alison J., Barbara Fister, and Margy MacMillan. *Information Literacy in the Age of Algorithms: Student Experiences with News and Information, and the Need for Change*. Project Information Research Institute, 2020, https://projectinfolit.org/publications/algorithm-study/

Horning, Alice S. "Now More Than Ever: Developing *Crafty Readers* in Writing Classes and Across the Curriculum." *Reading and Writing Instruction in the Twenty-First Century: Recovering and Transforming the Pedagogy of Robert Scholes*, edited by Ellen C. Carillo, 38–53. Utah State UP, 2021.

Hull, Glynda, and Mike Rose. "This Wooden Shack Place: The Logic of an Unconventional Reading." *College Composition and Communication*, vol. 41, no. 3, 1990, pp. 287–298.

Noble, Safiya Umoja. *Algorithms of Oppression: How Search Engines Reinforce Racism*. New York UP, 2018.

Rose, Mike. *Lives on the Boundary: The Struggles and Achievements of America's Educationally Underprepared*. Penguin Books, 1989.

Schick, Nina. *Deepfakes: The Coming Infocalypse*. 12/Tamang Ventures Limited, 2020.

Sullivan, Patrick, Howard Tinberg, and Sheridan Blau. *Deep Reading: Teaching Reading in the Writing Classroom*. NCTE, 2017.

Wineburg, Sam, Joel Breakstone, Nadav Ziv and Mark Smith. *Educating for Misunderstanding: How Approaches to Teaching Digital Literacy Make Students Susceptible to Scammers, Rogues, Bad Actors, and Hate Mongers*. Working Paper A-21322, 2020. Stanford History Education Group, https://purl.stanford.edu/mf412bt5333.

Wineburg, Sam, Joel Breakstone, Sarah McGrew, Mark Smith, and Teresa Ortega. "Lateral Reading on the Open Internet." 2021, Available at SSRN: https://ssrn.com/abstract=3936112 or http://dx.doi.org/10.2139/ssrn.3936112

Wolf, Maryanne. *Reader Come Home: The Reading Brain in a Digital World*. HarperCollins, 2018.

Alice S. Horning is professor emerita of writing and rhetoric/linguistics at Oakland University. Her research focuses on the intersection of reading and writing, concentrating on students' reading difficulties and how to address them in writing courses and across the disciplines. Her work has appeared in the major professional journals and in books published by Parlor Press and Hampton Press. Her most recent book is *Literacy Heroines: Women and the Written Word*, published by Peter Lang. She is the editor of the Studies in Composition and Rhetoric book series for Peter Lang.

Stepping Back to Step Forward: A Tribute to Mike Rose

Anthony Lince

The following article provides a narrative which details how Mike Rose positively influenced the author's practices, specifically as they relate to assessment and grading. The author first details his negative experiences with traditional grading as a high school teacher. Then, as he prepared to teach first-year writing courses at the college level, he discusses how Rose's ideas from Lives on the Boundary on the negative consequences of labels and judgments led him to Asao Inoue's work on labor-based grading. Lastly, he describe the positive impact that labor-based grading—and Mike Rose—has had on his teaching.

As I stepped into my first 10th grade English class as a student teacher, I was really excited. I was about to engage in the process of helping students discover powerful ideas through reading, and I'd assist them in critically thinking about important topics. Above all else, though, I was excited to teach writing. As a student in college, with the help of some truly wonderful English professors, I found my writerly voice, a discovery that allowed me to see just how powerful words can be. I wanted students—students like me who hated writing in high school, who feared putting words down on paper or screen for worry of sounding unintelligent—to see that they, too, had a writerly voice, albeit one that wasn't realized yet. Yes, the teaching of writing would be magical. Except, it mostly wasn't.

Whenever I wanted to talk to students about their writing—craft moves, purpose, expressing ideas—most would, inevitably, shift the conversations to focus on their grades, and, specifically, on the labels associated with those grades. F grades left students deflated and defeated—like they, themselves, were failures. D and C grades weren't much better and hardly inspired students to challenge themselves to write more, especially since those letters were accompanied with notions of being *remedial* and *average*.

I finished my student teaching feeling disappointed and unsure if I could make any real impact as an educator. Then, through a course reading in my teaching credential program, I discovered Mike Rose and his book *Lives on the Boundary*. Profound, brilliant, hopeful, and inspiring. Like many reading his work, I connected so strongly with his ideas, with his vision of a democratic education, one where every student belonged.

I completed my teaching credential program, and I decided to continue my schooling by pursuing an MA in English with an emphasis in rhetoric and writing studies. During my studies, I had an opportunity to teach first-year writing as a teaching associate. I took the opportunity. As I prepared my courses, a particular passage from *Lives on the Boundary*, because of my prior experiences in high school, kept on circling in my mind. Rose ended his book by arguing that the classroom can be a truly transformative place, but we, educators, need "a pedagogy that encourages us to step back and consider the threat of the standard classroom and that shows us, having stepped back, how to step forward to invite a student across the boundaries of that powerful room" (238). These words by Rose signaled to me that I had to really examine my previous practices as a teacher, and I had to do some thoughtful, meaningful, reflective work to try to find—and remove—the biggest threat that I had observed in the classroom. The answer, in my mind, was clear. The biggest threat to students was grades.

And even though Rose didn't speak specifically about grades and assessment, he did warn about the consequences of labels and judgments, which mainly stem from grades: "[T]hose judgments, accurate or not, affect the curriculum they receive, their place in the school, the way they're defined institutionally" (128). And students of color, multilingual students, students from low-income backgrounds—populations which, historically, have been in the institutional margins—often receive the harshest of judgments and labels. Students, as Rose powerfully noted, are sometimes powerless to stand outside of the definitions assigned to them through the various labels they've endured (128). And teachers, though try as they might, have a hard time moving beyond "established institutional perceptions" of students (128). By reading this in *Lives on the Boundary*, I started to gain an understanding that traditional assessment practices had to, in one way or another, be removed so as to not damage students' identities as learners. With this understanding, I realized that if I wanted myself and my students to move beyond reductive terms like remedial, illiterate, deficient—caused mainly by traditional assessment practices—I'd have to shift towards an alternative assessment method, one that was far more compassionate and equitable.

This was the "stepping back and stepping forward" work that had to be done. Therefore, with Rose's words guiding me, I searched for an assessment method that would allow me to see students as people, and one that would allow students to not worry about their identity through a grade or label. After reading Rose's work, I encountered Asao Inoue's *Labor-Based Grading Contracts Building Equity and Inclusion in the Compassionate Writing Classroom*. Inoue argues for teachers of writing to use labor-based grading, an alternative assessment practice that eschews letter grades, percentages, or any other evaluative mark, from students' writing and other work. The focus in this grading system is instead on providing students with meaningful written feedback, on being equitable, and antiracism (Inoue). In the article "Theorizing Failure in US Writing Assessments," Inoue also asserts that labor-based grading, because it doesn't use traditional measures of quality, could also potentially "avoid the damaging psychological effects . . . that grading by quality can cause many students, most notably students of color, working-class students, and multilingual students" (345). In many ways, reading Rose's work before reading Inoue's was perfect, because it primed me to see just how important it was to set up conditions in the classroom that weren't so focused on ranking and evaluating, on making judgments about people's abilities through a damaging mark. I was curious if labor-based grading would help honor students as people. It seemed like it did.

In my courses, labor-based grading allowed students to focus on their writing and not get so hung up on their grades. I remember in my high school classes, getting to the end of the year, and hoping that students had shifted their thinking and cared more about writing than grades. But that never happened. The pull of those evaluative marks was too strong, and students were always striving for the "perfect" grade, so they, themselves, could be perfect, perhaps ideas rooted in negative experiences. But in my college courses, those ideas didn't seem to enter the picture. In fact, some students, especially those who had been the most hurt by traditional grading practices, were able to forge new writerly identities, ones that weren't tethered to ideas of being deficient or inadequate. Students found, despite the negative labels previously assigned to them by academic institutions, they had a voice, and that they could use words to express powerful ideas, enact change, and tell moving stories. They were no longer burdened by the looming grade (and by the labels behind those grades) hanging over their shoulders. They could write and expect only feedback to help push their ideas forward.

Rose so often centered student voices in his scholarship, and I'd like to do the same here with a student's thoughts on labor-based grading from my class: "With labor-based grading, this is the first time I have ever cared about my writing." With other reflective comments on labor-based grading similar to this, it's evident to me that students felt like their words and ideas mattered, like they were being seen and heard—just as Rose surely saw his students.

Through his scholarship, Rose continually communicated his belief to educators, administrators, parents, and academic institutions about how students are so much more than the labels which are often attached to them. Instead of reducing students down to a quantitative mark, he hoped we might embrace education as a truly human endeavor. And to notice that every single student that walks through our door has their own potential to do something truly wonderful. In my courses, students and I are able to focus on writing without preoccupying ourselves with labels. In this way, I believe I am fulfilling, and extending, Rose's vision through my teaching.

Mike Rose no longer being with us leaves an immense hole in our educational landscape. Like many of us, I look to honor, celebrate, and extend his work in meaningful ways. I am forever thankful for Mike Rose and the positive impact he has had—and continues to have—on my teaching. I am grateful for his immense spirit and belief in the power of education. His kindness, generosity, and hopeful ideas will, no doubt, continue to influence our work in profound ways.

Works Cited

Inoue, Asao B. "Theorizing Failure in US Writing Assessments." *Research in the Teaching of English*, vol. 48, no. 3, 2014, pp. 330–52.

Inoue, Asao B. *Labor-Based Grading Contracts: Building Equity and Inclusion in the Compassionate Writing Classroom*. The WAC Clearinghouse, 2019.

Rose, Mike. *Lives on the Boundary: A Moving Account of the Struggles and Achievements of America's Educationally Underprepared*. Penguin Books. 2005.

Anthony Lince is a Latinx scholar, a student-centered teacher/instructor of English and first-year writing courses, and a qualitative teacher-researcher. His current research centers around equitable assessment practices.

A Different Kind of Hunger

Thomas Newkirk

Mike Rose's Lives on the Boundary *came out a few years after Richard Rodriguez's elegiac memoir* Hunger of Memory *and can be viewed as a powerful response. While Rose is sharply critical of the failure of modern universities to teach the under-prepared, he demonstrated, through his own story, that this instruction can happen if there is a more personal and intimate attempt to demystify academic work.*

Around 1990, we formed a reading group at University of New Hampshire and read together Richard Rodriguez's beautiful memoir *Hunger of Memory*. Rodriguez portrays himself as a Mexican-American version of the "scholarship boy" who was separated from the richness of his family culture but not really part of the mainstream academic world. The scholarship boy is stranded in a no-man's land, not really part of either world. There is a deep longing in *Hunger of Memory* for the warmth and closeness of the life Rodriguez has separated himself from, and could not retrieve—also an ambivalent feeling about the value of the trade he has made.

As we were discussing Rodriguez's book, someone asked what Mike Rose's take on *Hunger of Memory* would be. His own memoir, *Lives on the Boundary*, had just come out, and there were obvious parallels and clear differences. Mike, for example, was far less nostalgic about the life in LA he had left. Bob Connors, a member of our group, knew Mike and said, "Let's ask him." So he posed the question and by our next meeting Mike had responded.

As I recall, relying on my memory, Rose did not feel the alienation at the center of *Hunger of Memory* was inevitable. He believed that colleges and universities could be welcoming places, where there was at least the possibility of human connection and community. His own story was proof of that, the unforgettable portraits of his great teachers, like Dr. Ted Erlandson at Loyola:

> He worked as a craftsman works, with particulars, and he shuttled back and forth continually between print and voice, making me breathe my prose, making me hear the language I generated in silence. . . So Ted Erlandson's linguistic parenting felt just right: a modeling of grace until it slowly, slowly began to work itself into the way I shaped language. (Rose 55-56)

It can hardly get more intimate than that, Mike breathing his prose. It was exactly what he needed: explicit teaching that demystified academic expectations, modeling a form of precision that he found appealing. Mike's hunger was to enter this world as modeled for him by Erlandson and others.

Of course, big universities like University of California, Los Angeles rarely made this kind of teaching a high priority. Professors did not get tenure by working with underprepared students. The usual response to student difficulties has been to blame public schools for failing to prepare students—a form of complaint, Mike notes, that is as old as the modern university. Ambitious, smart but underprepared students, like Mike himself, often found themselves in huge, impersonal classes and suffering ego-shattering D's and F's when their high school skills were inadequate. Frequently, there was little effort, on the part of instructors, to unpack the skills or steps needed to be successful.

Mike, with his strong background in cognition, was so adept at this unpacking. Every assignment we give has a key verb that signifies a mental operation, often a complex and unfamiliar one. When we use terms like "analyze," "evaluate," and "discuss," we point to key academic skills, but we often don't illustrate how they are done. Too often, there is the assumption that just naming the mental processes is enough. In fact, it can be difficult for those of us, so familiar with these moves, to decenter and take the point of view of the student—who when confronted with these demands often default to awkward summarization. Almost every mistake I have made as a teacher comes from this failure to explain a process. Mike challenged us all to demystify these processes, to break them down—to teach them rather than to assume them.

Yet even as he exposed the failings of the university, he was, in his way, a traditionalist and an optimist. He respected, even revered, the core values of critical thinking and close reading. They had been liberating for him and could be for those students who struggled. There could be a place at the table for them as well.

I had never been to Mike's office, never attended a class, never had a conversation with him (though he did graciously provide a blurb to one of my books). But I can picture his office with unruly plants, soft, worn easy chairs, maybe a couch with some stuffing coming out, and the smell of fresh coffee in the air. I can imagine his classes with spicy food on a center table, laughter, and gregarious talk—settling down to discussion and at some point full attention on a sentence, read aloud, maybe multiple times, the words inspected, maybe altered.

I may not have this right, but it's my image and I'm holding to it.

Works Cited

Rose, Michael. *Lives on the Boundary: The Struggles, and Achievements of America's Underprepared.* Free Press, 1989.

Rodriguez, Richard. *Hunger of Memory: The Education of Richard Rodriguez.* Bantam, 1983

Thomas Newkirk is professor emeritus at the University of New Hampshire where he directed the first-year writing program and the New Hampshire Literacy Institutes, a summer program for teachers. He is the author of numerous books on literacy at all grade levels. His most recent text is *Writing Unbound: How Fiction Transforms Student Writers* (Heinemann. 2021). For seven years, he served as a member and as chair of his local school board.

Mike Rose: Helping All of Us Do Better

Kathleen Blake Yancey

Mike Rose left us with many legacies, three of which I highlight here: his re-conceptualization of school as part of the public; his reflection on both the human act of teaching and the promise of teaching more humanely; and the need for teachers to share widely what we have learned from our teaching.

I didn't know Mike Rose well, but I knew his work; I think every one of my generation did. Teaching pre-service teachers, I assigned *Lives on the Boundary*. Interested in models of composing, I read his work on writing blocks and cognition. Something of a student of linguistics and aware of the role metaphors play in shaping our understandings, I appreciated his point that in borrowing medical metaphors—as when we talked about *diagnosing* student writing—we pathologized writing. Reading his classroom research, with its intense focus on classroom conversation, I found it insightful, showing us what, *in medias res*, we often cannot otherwise see. Hearing his CCCC Exemplar address's exhortation that we take our work public, I thought it brilliant. But perhaps most of all, I appreciated the way Mike always saw the human in all of us.

Mike Rose wasn't a typical WPA, of course. He directed a writing program early in his career, but left the post pretty quickly, never to return; he didn't publish in *WPA: Writing Program Administration*; he didn't serve on the Executive Board or as an officer for the Council of Writing Program Administrators. Put simply, he didn't inhabit the role of the WPA as we ordinarily construe it. And yet, his legacy, at least implicitly, raises several continuing questions for WPAs, three of which I explore here.

First: *What is the role of the public sphere in WPA work?*

Mike Rose's philosophy of education was located squarely in the public sphere, as he explained on his own blog:

> If I had to sum up the philosophical thread that runs through my work, it would be this: A deep belief in the ability of the common person, a commitment to educational, occupational, and cultural opportunity to develop that ability, and an affirmation of public institutions and the public sphere as vehicles for nurturing and expressing that ability.

Jeffersonian in spirit but situated in and informed by 20th and 21st century contexts, Mike's common person wasn't Jefferson's property-holding white man, but rather *all* common people, kaleidoscopic in their dazzlingly diverse colors, shapes, and sizes. Mike's common person necessarily had ability, one entitled to support; after all, providing such support, nurturing ability, was the responsibility of public institutions as well as the pleasure and the opportunity of the public sphere.

Second: *How do we share our experience of teaching writing with the world?*

This question, related to but different than the first, asks us more directly to think about how we make our experience available to others in the world. As Mike's work itself illustrates, he believed in writing for various publics: the community of teachers of writing, certainly, but also—and perhaps more importantly—the larger democratic community. He made this very clear in his 2012 CCCC Exemplar Address as he bid us to share our expertise and make connections with the wider world.

> Seek the public sphere. Write and talk about what you do to as wide an audience as you can. ... Frame a career that along with the refereed article and research monograph includes and justifies the opinion piece and the blog commentary - and craft a writing style that is knowledgeable and keenly analytic and has a public reach. (543)

Some seven years later in a "Bonus Episode" of the inaugural *Pedagogue* podcast, Mike reiterated his point even more strongly in his response to Shane Wood's question about how higher education is represented: "Who Says What (And What Gets Told) About Higher Education?"

> So I guess my answer is, like Sisyphus, it may be a near impossible task, but we just kind of keep coming at it and keep coming at it in every possible way that we have of conveying the reality of the work we do and the people who are in our classrooms. Maybe what we're talking about here is the need for all of us who do this kind of work, regardless of where we do it, to see ourselves not only as teachers, and possibly as scholars of writing and rhetoric, but also as writers or communicators or rhetoricians.

Here, then, in asking us to open our classroom doors even more, Mike creates a new public teaching-related role for all of us.

Third: *How Can a Practice of Critical Reflection, Located in the "We" of All Teachers, Benefit Our Students?*

Mike Rose's disposition was critically reflective. Reflection, of course, can take a myriad of forms, from exploration and synthesis to self-assessment and theory-building. Despite these differences, however, at its core reflection is a meaning-making activity. The specific meaning Mike made in his reflections took the form of *critical reflection*, one especially sensitive to larger structures, particularly those embedded in power relations. And as Stephen Brookfield explains, critical reflection is an especially helpful practice for teachers.

> Reflection becomes critical when it has two distinct purposes. The first is to understand how considerations of power undergird, frame and distort educational processes and interactions. The second is to question assumptions and practices that seem to make our teaching lives easier but actually work against our own long-term best interests. (8)

With his co-authors in "Remediation as Social Construct: Perspectives from an Analysis of Classroom Discourse," Mike demonstrates such critical reflection through looking at the classroom, especially the "remedial" classroom, and in doing so, carefully plotting relationships between a small classroom study and the larger contexts in which it is situated and to which it responds. In a classroom discussion leading to instructions for a formal writing assignment, a student discourses surprisingly, interrupting it and—worse—taking the class discussion off (the teacher's) track. The teacher sees someone not ready for college; Mike sees a student enriching the conversation while, admittedly, taking the conversation to a topic that (1) the teacher hadn't anticipated and (2) isn't directly related to the assignment. Although the teacher is correct on both counts, as Mike points out, excluding the student's contribution means that "Maria's moment for contributing a piece of knowledge is lost, and so is an opportunity for the class to consider an important issue" (Hull et al. 309).

Drawing a larger lesson from this individual one, and despite our best intentions, Mike says, we teachers can too easily think of student efforts as motivated by deficits, can too often fail to observe what students do bring to school with them, rather than what we want them to bring. Moreover, he understands this tendency as a problem we *all* need to confront and address. How, he asks,

> can we as teachers and researchers examine our assumptions about remediation and remedial writing and remedial students? How can we be alert to deficit explanations for the difficulties that students experience in our classrooms? We have four suggestions: remembering teacher development, attending to classroom discourse, making macro-micro connections, and rethinking the language of cultural difference. (316)

These four suggestions seem as valid, necessary, and helpful today as they did in 1991 when Mike was outlining them, and one of them, of course, especially belongs in the WPA wheelhouse: *teacher development*. Pointing to a 1981 special issue of *the Journal of Basic Writing* focusing on preparing teachers for remedial writing classrooms and featuring a host of well-known WPAs—including Harvey Wiener, Richard Gebhardt, Charles Moran, Donald McQuade and Marie Ponsot—Mike reminds us that "We need to spend some time thinking about teacher development--not just what knowledge to impart about writing, but how to develop the ability to question received assumptions about abilities and performance, how to examine the thinking behind the curricula we develop and the assessments we make" (318). Indeed, as Mike argues, all teachers, novice and expert, benefit from examining assumptions, especially as we continue to widen the classroom door to student contributions.[1] We might even think of teaching, Mike says, "as an ongoing flow of moments of invitation and moments of denial. The better, the more effective the teaching, the richer and more frequent the moments of invitation, encouragement, and assistance" (318).

In this article about an individual classroom, about teachers writ large, and about teacher development, Mike and his colleagues emphasize the community of teachers through the repeated use of the term we; it appears 151 times. Given that frequency, it's worth pausing to consider who the we includes, as the following excerpt suggests.

> *We write this paper* believing that, however great the distance our profession has come in understanding the students and the writing we call "re- medial," *we have not yet come far enough in critically examining our assumptions about our students' abilities—assumptions which both shape the organization of remedial programs and orient daily life in remedial classrooms.* Engaging in such an examination is not so easy, perhaps because *as teachers of remedial writing, we have good intentions* .... (299; italics mine)

A first we is that of the authors: "We write this paper. . . ."

A second we is that of the field: "we have not yet come far enough in critically examining our assumptions about our students' abilities--assumptions which both shape the organization of remedial programs and orient daily life in remedial classrooms."

And a third we is, quite simply, teachers: "as teachers of remedial writing, we have good intentions . . ."

These separate we's overlap: the classroom teacher participates in the field by virtue of her practice, as do we all. Notably, there's no hierarchy here, no dichotomy, no experienced teacher vs. novice, no enlightened teacher vs. a deficit-oriented one. And perhaps most importantly, there is no blame: we all have such assumptions, drawing on them is a natural practice, and we can do better. Put another way: community members participate in overlapping communities of teachers who, working together, can focus our efforts on increasing *moments of invitation, encouragement, and assistance.*

Interestingly, too, the article itself is positioned not so much as an argument, but rather as an invitation to collective reflection through which teachers can examine their "basic assumptions" and consider ways of changing them, "building from a different ground":

> Our hope, then, is that this paper will be an occasion to reflect on the ways we, teachers, can inadvertently participate in the social construction of attitudes and beliefs about remediation which may limit the learning that takes place in our classrooms, and to consider some ways in which we can begin to examine these basic assumptions, building from a different ground our notions about our students' abilities and the nature of literacy learning. (300)

These three questions are important for all of us who teach writing as they are for WPAs, who teach writing and teachers of writing; who design programs; who communicate across campuses; and, as per Mike Rose, who reach out to the wider world. He cautions us that in doing all this, we do better by connecting with others than by separating from them, given that we all participate in the same common good.

Located in three key legacies–a reflective conceptualization of the public; the human act of teaching and the promise of teaching more humanely; and the need to share that experience widely–Mike Rose's legacy focused, quite simply, smartly, and generously, on helping all of us do better.

Note

1. Some programs in higher education are engaging in such practices. See, for example, Oregon State University's Insight Resume (reported in Yancey). See also University of Buffalo's ePortfolio program; student grades, achievement of outcomes, *and* student perceptions of learning are collected and developed for program enhancement. This latter program is also unusual in that it (1) includes artifacts from outside the institution and (2) permits evidence of, and reflection on, student failure. See Kohler et al., and Emerson and Reid.

WORKS CITED

Brookfield, Stephen. *Becoming a Critically Reflective Teacher*, first edition. Jossey-Bass. 1995.

Emerson, Cheryl Emerson and Alex Reid. "Integrative Learning and ePortfolio Networks." *Portfolio-as-Curriculum: Diverse Models and Practices*, edited by Kathleen Blake Yancey, Stylus 2019, pp. 203–233.

Hull, Glynda, Mike Rose, Kay Losey Fraser and Marisa Castellano. "Remediation as Social Construct: Perspectives from an Analysis of Classroom Discourse." *College Composition and Communication*, vol. 42, no. 3, 1991, pp. 299–329.

Kohler, Jeffrey J. and Carol Van Zile-Tam. "Metacognitive Matters: Assessing the High-Impact Practice of a General Education Capstone ePortfolio." *International Journal of ePortfolio*, vol. 10, no. 1, 2020, pp 33–43.

Rose, Mike. "CCCC Exemplar Address." *College Composition and Communication*, vol. 64, no. 3, 2013, pp. 542–544.

—. "Who Says What (And What Gets Told) About Higher Education?" *Pedagogue*. 2019. Available https://www.pedagoguepodcast.com/uploads/4/1/9/0/41908851/pedagogue_bonus_mike_rose.pdf

Yancey, Kathleen Blake. "College Admissions and the Insight Resume: Writing, Reflection, and Students' Lived Curriculum as a Site of Equitable Assessment." *Race and Writing Assessment*, edited by Asao Inoue and Mya Poe, Peter Lang, 2012, pp. 171–87.

Kathleen Blake Yancey, Kellogg W. Hunt Professor of English and Distinguished Research Professor Emerita, has led several literacy organizations, including the Council of Writing Program Administrators. She focuses her research on composition studies generally; on students' transfer of writing knowledge and practice; on cultural studies of everyday writing; on writing assessment, especially print and electronic portfolios; and on the intersections of culture, literacy and technologies. In addition to co-founding the journal *Assessing Writing* and co-editing it for seven years, she is a past editor of *College Composition and Communication*. She has also authored, edited, or co-edited sixteen scholarly books as well as over 100 articles and book chapters. Yancey is the recipient of numerous awards, among them the CCCC Exemplar Award and the National Council of Teachers of English Squire Award, "given to an NCTE member who has had a transforming influence and has made a lasting intellectual contribution to the profession."

Keeping the Faith: Rediscovering the Hope of Mike Rose

Julie Lindquist

This essay argues that Mike Rose's work created a distinctive pathway for writing program administration. Rose understood education as a deeply human project—one steeped in questions of equity and educational principles. A return to Rose's work simultaneously demonstrates the persistence of questions regarding what counts as education as well as how inclusion and exclusion are fostered by our attempts to define "higher" education.

Let me start by saying that the invitation to write this short piece reflecting on Mike Rose and his work came at exactly the right time. I'll confess that these past two years have left me feeling fairly discouraged, and more than a little bit cynical, about the possibilities of education. When it comes to the promise of education—of, as Shane Wood reminds us in this collection, quoting Mike, that "grand human enterprise"—I needed to feel hopeful again. In my conversations with teachers of first-year writing in the very large writing program I direct, I've been hearing more and more from them about their struggles to keep the students who show up—or not—in their classes invested, present, and engaged. At the same time, much has been said and written recently about the crisis of faith the pandemic has occasioned. A recent piece in the *Chronicle of Higher Education* (McMurtrie), takes up the question of why students seem so disengaged at present, positing, ultimately, that students may simply be unable to sustain their faith in the possible futures that they once believed education would secure. For me, especially in this moment, the act of reflecting on Mike's life and contributions, and reading these authors writing about Mike's impacts and his example, has been an entirely hopeful endeavor. Especially in my life as a WPA, in these times of trouble, uncertainty, and crises of faith, the experience of spending time with Mike and his work—and with others who are also spending time with his work—has gone a long way toward restoring my faith in the work of education, and in the power of the community of fellow educators who labor alongside me, even from a distance.

We don't know for sure what Mike would have said about the pain and difficulty students and teachers are currently feeling, at *this* moment, two years and some months after COVID-19 arrived on the US scene in March 2020. I have a feeling, though, that he would have met the moment with his usual compassion, and would have offered a message of hope for his fellow human beings, and some ideas for a way forward. The thing about

Mike Rose is that he truly believed in the project of education, for all its flaws, limitations, and (even) its sins. His writing over the years is an expansive body of work that demonstrates—regardless of purpose, audience, and venue—that he never lost faith in the transformative potential of schooling, however much he saw it as an imperfect project. In fact, Mike devoted a life to inquiring into the function of education as a sorting mechanism, and he did so in the service of remediating its potential as an equalizing force. I, like many others, saw hope in—and felt *seen* in—*Lives on the Boundary,* which I had the opportunity to read in graduate school, when I was—like many others—questioning my place in the world of academics.

Then, as luck would have it, Mike was in the audience of my very first-ever CCCC panel presentation in 1992, and he approached me after the talk to voice his appreciation and encouragement for my ideas about language and class identity. That affirmation was more meaningful than I am sure he ever knew. It came at a time when I was deeply unconvinced that, as a first-generation student, I had anything of particular value to offer—other than, perhaps, my account of my own struggles to find a place in higher education. Mike helped me to see how that experience could be a powerful position from which to do research on literacy and learning, and how *that* could be a real contribution.

At this moment, twenty-five years into my career, and in my second go-round as a writing program administrator, I find myself in a good position to reflect on Mike's influence as a model of how to do the work those of us who lead general education writing programs must, necessarily, do. I have come to understand WPA work (especially now, in the third year of pandemic time) as operating almost exclusively in the domain of *wicked problems*. In the by-now-famous formulation of design theorists Horst Rittel and Melvin Webber, a "wicked problem" names a situation in which there are only forms of compromise under difficult conditions, a kind of problem that "will generate waves of consequences over an extended—virtually an unbounded—period of time," and in which "the next day's consequences of the solution may yield utterly undesirable repercussions" (163). From this perspective, WPA work is a predicament that is, whatever else it may be, relational, a practice of negotiation for which the pedagogical work—and the work of translation between interested parties—is ongoing. The past three years, under (pandemic-related) conditions of institutional disruption and with the general erosion of trust that comes with isolation, negotiating the tricky relational territory of educational spaces has been especially difficult, and never more critical. Mike's distinctive ability to translate the work of teaching and learning writing to other audiences reminds us not only of how important it is for WPAs to make the work of literacy education intelligible to various publics, but also how to be nimble and persistent pedagogues in relation to these publics. As a public intellectual, Mike made it his mission (and his practice) to talk to those outside out discipline–fellow educators, policymakers, other publics—who are also invested in education, and who have a stake in how it proceeds.

Mike's unfailingly human, and humane, way of seeing others is one of the things—in addition to his deeply embodied sense of the stakes and difficulties of education, and his exceptional talent as a storyteller—that enabled him to do this kind of translation work. You will have noticed that Mike's generous availability to others is a theme that surfaces across the essays in this issue. Many of the authors in this collection have stories of their encounters with Mike, and their discovery of his genuine humility. These stories of interactions with Mike—conversations in the passages and transitions and byways of educational spaces, and of everyday life—offer a testament to Mike's preferred means of engagement. Perhaps because of his own persistent sense of having landed in higher education as an outsider, Mike never underestimated the value of a hallway conversation, and never overestimated the value of the merely didactic.

Like many of those whose writings are collected here, I, too, had an experience of Mike as a fellow human. In fact, I had the astonishing good fortune to call him a friend. Our relationship developed through our mutual experience of being first-generation academics from the working class, educators whose interest in the work was related to our commitment to the value of access for students who, as Mike famously observed in "I Just Wanna Be Average," struggled to find a way in. I was enormously gratified, early in my career (and in the darkest hour of my impostor syndrome), that Mike paid attention to my writings on working-class experience and class culture, and--even more remarkable!—found them to be of value. We had long conversations about teaching, writing, and life in general; I learned, via one of these conversations, that a diner called Norm's Restaurant in Los Angeles, where I had worked for a time as a teenager, had been the place where his own mother, Rose (whose embodied expertise Mike chronicled in his book about the intelligence of forms of everyday labor, *The Mind At Work*) had worked for many years. It so often seemed as if we were fellow travelers, connected by the path we'd shared, and by our commitment to the same destination. In reading the pieces in this collection, I'm not at all surprised to find that I am far from alone in my experiences with, and observations of, Mike's interactions with others, and in the grace he always, without exception, extended to these others—colleagues, admirers, strangers.

In explaining to other admirers and students of Mike's work–others who had not had the good fortune to meet him–what Mike was like, I like to tell this story: At CCCCs in 2009, Mike and I had planned to meet up in the lobby of the conference hotel, and then head off to a local bar to grab a drink and catch up. We'd found each other in the lobby of the San Francisco Hilton—or rather, I found him, surrounded, as always, with fans who had spotted and encircled him. After Mike was finally able to disengage and take his leave, we began to make our way toward the exit. On (what became a very protracted) journey across the hotel lobby, it seemed that Mike could only make a few feet of progress in any direction before being stopped and greeted by yet another person who had found his work to be meaningful in some way. I recall that he engaged every single person who approached him. Every single one. And he engaged them with warmth, generosity, and genuine curiosity, as a fellow human from whom he had something important to learn. Like all brilliant teachers, he was never condescending, never didactic, never enamored of the imagined virtue of his own expertise. Instead, he was generous with his attention, believed in the power of the learner's mind, and trusted that the rest would follow.

Beyond the value of his writings about education, and the values he himself embodied, Mike also gifted us with an example of what a career as a professional academic—and in particular, as a theorist and practitioner of literacy and learning—could look like. Some fifteen years ago (!), I was invited to write a review of a new volume of Mike's collected works, *An Open Language: Selected Writing on Literacy, Learning, and Opportunity*. That invitation, too, was a gift, as it gave me the opportunity to sit with a body of work in a dwelling-in (rather than looking-across) way I typically didn't have the occasion to do. I noted in that piece ("Looking Back at the Road Ahead") that Mike's writing addressed "cognitive processes, writing programs, composition textbooks, schools, workplaces, literacy theory, and educational policy." I also wrote that Mike approached these subjects with "a fully packed kit of methodological equipment, from protocol analysis to case study to long-term participant observation," and that his body of work thus far showed him "tacking back and forth between macro and micro views of writing and literacy, between groups and individuals, between in- and out-of-school settings" (72). Spending time with Mike's work over time revealed just how little he was motivated by academic opportunism, aspirationalism, or the seductions of extractive research. Rather, his imagination was animated by the experience (his own, and those of others) of being an educational subject (and agent), institutional predicaments of education, and common narratives of schools, schooling, and students. I remember thinking, as I worked on that review, just how rare Mike's approach to learning and scholarly production really was. Of *An Open Language*, I wrote:

> For all the research and scholarship we produce, it isn't often that a single work allows us to experience the expansive terrain of composition studies as a field of inquiry and practice, to sit in the passenger's seat of the car as it bumps along over the ground in the shallow tracks of an emerging road, seeing what the driver sees and listening to him think aloud about how to go next. For those of us just starting out, Rose's work helps us to envision something we have no resources to yet imagine: how, indeed, can a single life of inquiry in this field unfold? For those of us who have been working in the field for many years, the book is in fact an important retrospective on how the road might once have looked as it emerged *then* and *there*, encouraging us to reflect on the meaning of paths made and roads not taken (71).

Mike's particular journey, it seemed to me, defined the landscape of the field in which we worked, even as it marked out an altogether distinctive pathway. But then, if you saw (as Mike did) education as a deeply human project, it follows that you would be inclined to be attentive to what the humans engaged in the project of education—as agents or subjects—might have to teach you. You would ask the question, always, what does it mean to be a human being who is implicated in education? What kinds of humans are implicated, and which ways? To what effects? And how can education be (re)conceived as a (more) humane endeavor? I feel Mike's death a loss not only of an exceptional human, but also of a future. It's impossible not to wonder what more might Mike have gifted us, in these terribly difficult ("challenging," as administrators like to say) times. Indeed, it is possible to identify a throughline from many of our current conversations relevant to equity and inclusion back to the basic principles of social justice Mike articulated as educational principles in, and ever since the publication of, *Lives on the Boundary*.

Mike Rose has given us so very much. In spite of that—and also because of it—the news of his passing felt like yet another one of 2021's malicious turns of fate. In his November 2020 blog post, Mike wrote:

> In this season of giving thanks and expressing gratitude, there is much I am thankful for.
>
> I am thankful for you, the readers of this blog, and thankful for all my readers in any medium.
>
> To have something you've written read by others is a great honor.

I'm thankful for the expulsion from the presidency of my country a cloven-footed, grotesquely evil man.

I'm thankful for my many friendships and deep relationships, which sustain me and give my life profound meaning.

I'm thankful for teaching, which I fell into by dumb luck at 24. Teaching defines me and gives my life purpose, and I am fortunate beyond words to love it as much now as I did upon discovering it.

I'm thankful to be able to write—it gives me an absorbing craft and a way to be in the world.

Me, I'm thankful that *we* had, in our lives and in our hearts, this example of an intellectual leader who had the grace and humility to be thankful to all those to whom he gave so much.

Works Cited

Colombo, Gary, Robert Cullen, and Bonnie Lisle. *Rereading America: in Cultural Contexts for Critical Thinking and Writing*. Bedford Books of St. Martin's Press, 1995.

Lindquist, Julie. "Review: Looking Back at the Road Ahead." *College English,* vol. 70, no.1,2007,: pp. 70-78.

McMurtrie, Beth. "A 'Stunning' Level of Disconnection: Professor are Reporting Record Numbers of Students Checked Out, Stressed Out, Unsure of Their Future." *Chronicle of Higher Education,* 5 Apr., 2022, https://www.chronicle.com/article/a-stunning-level-of-student-disconnection

Rittel, Horst, and M. M. Webber. "Dilemmas in a General Theory of Planning." *Policy Sciences, vol.* 4, 1973, pp. 155–69.

Rose, Mike. "I Just Wanna be Average." *Rereading America: Cultural Contexts for Critical Thinking and Writing*, 1990, pp. 161-72

—. *Lives on the Boundary : A Moving Account of the Struggles and Achievements of America's Educationally Underprepared*. Penguin Books, 2005.

—. *An Open Language: Selected Writings on Literacy, Learning, and Opportunity*. MacMillan Press, 2006.

—. "Thank You." Mike Rose's Blog, November 2021. http://mikerosebooks.blogspot.com/2020/11/thank-you.html

—. *The Mind at Work: Valuing the Intelligence of the American Worker*. New York: Viking, 2004.

Julie Lindquist is a professor of writing, rhetoric, and American cultures at Michigan State University. She has been the director of the first-year writing program at Michigan State University since 2012. Her scholarly interests have been related to language, class, culture, and educational access. She has published books and articles on the relationship of language and culture to literacy and writing pedagogy.

Listening to Mike Rose: Education Is a Grand Human Enterprise

Shane A. Wood

Mike Rose dedicated his life to teaching and writing about education. He influenced teachers and students across the nation, and the author was fortunate to get to know him over the last two years. What stood out in their conversations were Rose's curiosity and commitment to exploring human nature.

This is a vignette, a short story of when I got the chance to *listen* to Mike Rose. There are a lot of people who were closer to Mike, who knew him for a longer period of time, who had deeper relationships, better friendships, and a greater understanding of who he was than me. There are a lot of folks who had him as a teacher, friend, mentor, confidant, who knew him intimately, got to learn from him, and got to experience his compassion at greater depths. And there's a lot of us who read his books and personal blog posts and words in *The Washington Post*, or heard his talks, lectures, presentations, and were charmed by his charisma and enthusiasm for teaching.

My story starts on April 18, 2019, when I emailed Mike to ask if he'd be interested in being on a podcast about teachers talking writing called *Pedagogue*.

Mike Rose—a superstar in education.

My email—a cold call.

I didn't know, at least in that moment, that Mike's generosity exceeded his well-known academic career and status. He responded within 24 hours: "I would be honored."

Over the next two years (2019-2021) Mike and I talked quite a bit. Sometimes we chatted about teaching, sometimes about writing, and sometimes about life. I still laugh when he called on a Saturday morning in September while I was mowing the backyard to ask who he could send copies of *Back to School* to and in return, said he'd mail me a bottle of Johnnie Walker Blue.

Mike Rose was truly one of a kind. You could hear gratitude in his voice. He spoke with tenderness. He carried a spirit of curiosity and compassion. His generosity was boundless. Most of the time I felt like he didn't even know the extent of his impact on teachers, students, colleagues. I never really understood that part of Mike.

In fall 2019, he emailed me again because he wanted to do a short episode that extended his thoughts in *Back to School* on "second-chancers" and "nontraditional" college students. He was hoping to "capture the texture of people's lives…that we rarely see represented in policy or news reports." From my point-of-view, in those short two years, Mike was committed to peeling back the layers of education and humanity. He saw education and humanity as intertwined, and he was going to unknot it like yarn.

And in our conversations, he would start with humanity. He would rather tell stories about teachers and mentors, like Jack MacFarland, Ben Campos, and Rosalie Naumann, to name a few. He'd rather talk about how they encouraged and inspired him. He'd rather talk about Rose Meraglio Rose (Rosie), his mom who quit school in 7th grade to care for her family. He'd rather talk about her intellectual curiosity as a career waitress and her interactions with customers. So much so that he wrote about it in the first chapter of *The Mind at Work: Valuing the Intelligence of the American Worker*. Last but not least, he'd rather tell story after story about his students in elementary school, adult education courses, tutoring centers and mentoring programs, and colleges and universities, and talk about their lives and how special it was to teach.

Mike shared his first teaching experience with me on our first phone call. At 24 years old he joined a program called the Teacher Corps. He was placed in El Monte, California, and he spent all summer with a team of people getting to know the community: "I mean we met everybody. We met the priest, we met the mechanic, we met parents, we met kids, we met teachers" (*Pedagogue*, Episode 1). After spending the summer in the El Monte community, he walked into the classroom as a teacher for the first-time teaching 6th graders, mostly working-class White and Latino students. He said he was nervous, "I was green. I was young. I didn't know what the hell I was doing, and was excited to see what would happen" (*Pedagogue*, Episode 1).

Mike started teaching with the same timidity I imagine the rest of us felt our first-time in the classroom. Maybe that's why he never felt out-of-touch even with all his achievements and successes. It felt like Mike always remembered where he came from and how he ended up in the classroom. He was reflective and spoke so highly of his own teachers and mentors. Which was relatable. He believed teaching was a gift. Which was inspirational. In December 2020, Mike emailed me, "Thank God for the writing and students." That's Mike. Grateful, and with his mind on students. Kevin Dettmar, American cultural critic and writer for *The New Yorker*, put it this way, "[Mike] modelled a deep compassion that asked teachers to understand students as whole people" ("The Teacher Who Changed How We Teach Writing").

Seeing and understanding students as "whole people" felt like Mike's modus operandi. He loved talking about the purpose of education and how when you teach you learn more about what it means to be human. He told me, "There's something profoundly special it seems to me about having the good fortune to teach because you really are participating with other people in their development" (*Pedagogue*, Episode 1). He understood how *listening* was essential to teaching: "I can't tell you what a fundamental pedagogical skill listening has become for me over the decades… I mean think of it, how many people do you know that really listen to you when you sit down to talk with them?" (*Pedagogue*, Episode 1).

Mike also modeled what it meant to be a great listener. He encouraged us to pursue a fuller definition of education as its connected to human nature, and this starts by listening. His writings demonstrate this commitment to exploring the human condition, specifically issues of social class, race, language, and economics. *Lives on the Boundary*, perhaps his most well-known book, interconnected these issues and represented his own educational journey. It also showed the profound impact dedicated teachers can make on the lives of students. What stands out about *Lives of the Boundary*, and other books like *Back to School* and *Possible Lives*, is that education can't be separated from intellectual, social, civic, moral, and aesthetic realities.

In other words, Mike taught me a lot about education and humanity. That classrooms are never *just* classrooms. Students are never *just* students. Teachers are never *just* teachers. He gave me a greater perspective on identity and on politics, and how reading and writing are nuanced activities. He reminded me about the structures working within and beyond our lives shaping what we see and do as administrators, teachers, and students. He helped magnify our realities and revealed what it meant to be on the margins, working-class, overlooked, underprepared, historically disadvantaged.

He writes about this in *Back to School*, where he describes spending years interviewing students at a two-year college. He explores how "nontraditional" students balance education, social and political realities, and economic challenges. There's a moment when a student named Ray asks Mike what he's doing there in that classroom, in that specific context. Mike replies, "To study programs like this one because we need to know more about them to convince our politicians that we need more of them" (116). Ray responds, "It's the teacher that really makes a difference . . . he treats us like we're people" (116). I think about this brief exchange between Mike and Ray a lot, and ponder what it means for us in education, whether that be as writing program administrators or teachers. I think Mike reminds us that what we see "depends on where you sit, and for how long" (115). Wherever we are, and whatever we're doing, we can't lose sight of the *humanness* of our work—that's a lesson Mike reminded me time and time again in our conversations.

On January 19, 2021, we talked for the last time. I was finishing a book called *Teachers Talking Writing* that was connected to *Pedagogue* and the wonderful conversations I had with teachers and scholars on the podcast. Mike was in the first chapter, of course, and I asked for a bio. His last lines read,

> I have been in education for the long haul, and it has given my life great meaning . . . education is a grand human enterprise, on a par with medicine or theology in the insight it gives us into the human condition, our struggles and our achievements. I feel so, so lucky to have found this work.

I think it's safe to say that Mike spent his life sitting, listening, and learning from students. He examined the small particles of life—all the material, mental, emotional, political, social, and physical realities. Which is why Mike would probably ask us to consider how we are making a difference with our stories and with our voices. He would probably encourage us to think about who we are writing to/for and would gently remind us "to see ourselves not only as teachers . . . but also as writers or communicators or rhetoricians" (*Pedagogue Bonus*).

Education is a grand human enterprise. So, how are we humanizing what we do? How are we communicating the grand human enterprise of education? Our future work should start with these questions, and we should spend more time sitting and listening. And of course, we should use these experiences sitting and listening to shape larger conversations about reading, writing, literacy, teaching, students, and education.

Just like Mike.

Works Cited

Dettmar, Kevin. "The Teacher Who Changed How We Teach Writing." *The New Yorker*. October 14, 2021.

Pedagogue. "Episode 1: Mike Rose (pt. 1)." Podcast: Published May 9, 2021.

Pedagogue. "Pedagogue Bonus: Who Says What (And What Gets Told) About Higher Education? (w/Mike Rose)." Podcast. Published December 29, 2019.

Rose, Mike. *Lives on the Boundary: A Moving Account of the Struggles and Achievements of America's Educationally Underprepared*. Free Press, 1989.

—. *Possible Lives: The Promise of Public Education in America*. Houghton Mifflin Company, 1995.

—. *The Mind at Work: Valuing the Intelligence of the American Worker*. Viking Penguin, 2004.

—. *Back to School: Why Everyone Deserves a Second Chance at Education*. The New Press, 2012.

Shane A. Wood is assistant professor of English at the University of Southern Mississippi, where he teaches first-year writing, digital literacies, and technical writing. He received his BA in English from Western Kentucky University, MA in English from Fresno State, and PhD in rhetoric and composition from the University of Kansas. His research interests include writing assessment, teacher response, and multimodal pedagogy. His work has appeared in journals such as *The Journal of Writing Assessment*, *WPA: Writing Program Administration*, and *Computers and Composition*.

Mike Rose: Insights from the Classroom

Mike Palmquist

While many of the articles in this special issue focus on contributions Mike Rose made through his scholarly work, this essay provides a discussion of his work in the classroom. Drawing on a graduate seminar taught in Fall 1986, when Rose was serving as a visiting professor at Carnegie Mellon University, the article explores key aspects of Rose's approach to designing and teaching a course.

I met Mike Rose in August 1986, when I was a new graduate student in the doctoral program at Carnegie Mellon University and Mike had joined the faculty for the year as a visiting professor. The class I took from him that fall and the conversations we had over the course of that year shaped who I would become as a scholar and, even more directly, as a teacher. In retrospect, the time I spent with Mike played a critical role in launching a career that I had given little consideration to pursuing prior to my decision to apply to Carnegie Mellon's rhetoric program the previous spring.

I'm certainly not alone in recognizing the impact of Mike Rose's work on teaching and learning. The articles in this special issue offer powerful testimony to the enduring legacy of his scholarly work, collegiality, and generosity. They underscore what those of us who know Mike and his scholarship (I am still struggling with the verb tense) have long understood: that he gave willingly to his students, to his colleagues (and his notion of colleague is broad and inclusive), and to the field. His scholarship has shaped the teaching of writing for more than four decades. His books and articles have expanded the reach of writing studies far beyond our discipline. And the example he set as a caring and committed teacher and researcher, borne of his own early struggles with learning and enhanced by the connections he made with so many of us, will long be held up as an ideal that many of us will strive to emulate, even as we see, through the words he shared with us, how difficult that will be to achieve.

Mike understood well that we can move forward best as a community—or, perhaps, as many communities with congruent goals. He grounds much of his writing in the connections we share as individuals and as a society, in research reports such as "Rigid Rules, Inflexible Plans, and the Stifling of Language: A Cognitivist Analysis of Writers Block" (1980), historically grounded analyses such as "The Language of Exclusion: Writing Instruction at the University" (1985), commentaries in *Inside Higher Ed* and *The Chronicle of Higher Education*, and in the books for which he is best known and which so clearly show his connections to individuals and the challenges they face, such as *Lives on the Boundary* (1989), *The Mind at Work: Valuing the Intelligence of the American Worker* (2004), and *Why School? Reclaiming Education for All of Us* (2012). His focus on individual struggle illuminates the larger challenges we face as educators and as a society. In a way, Mike Rose can be seen as a series of moments—each important, each enduring, and each resonant of the challenges we face as teachers, learners, and as members of a complex and often difficult society.

While attention to the impact of Mike's work on the field, his generous interactions with colleagues, and his concern for his students runs through the articles in this collection, what isn't as apparent is his impact on the many students he taught over his long and productive career. In August 1986, I became one of those students when I enrolled in Mike's graduate seminar at Carnegie Mellon. I sometimes joke that I'm an accidental professor, having given up a career as a professional writer to follow my wife from the Twin Cities to Pittsburgh, where she had enrolled in Carnegie Mellon's master's program in professional writing. I was naïve, uninformed, and unprepared for what I would face, so the idea of enrolling in CMU's doctoral program didn't faze me—at first. I thought, for example, that working as a graduate teaching assistant implied that I would be supporting an experienced instructor—not teaching my own class. I was unaware that getting a master's degree before enrolling in a doctoral program would have been a good idea. And my understanding of what it means to write and to be a writer were more aligned with expressivism than the cognitive rhetoric that was a central concern of the program.

In many ways, the faculty I worked with that first semester offered me a lifeline. I was in over my head, especially when I contrasted my preparation with that of the other members of my entering class. But Chris Neuwirth, Richard Young, and Mike Rose helped me avoid drowning in a wave of new and often conflicting ideas. By the end of that semester, I had learned not only enough to understand our then-emerging field but had also begun to understand, through their example, what it meant to teach well.

I don't remember as clearly as I'd like the content of the discussions we had in Mike's seminar. Although the readings he assigned were ultimately important to my development as a scholar, my lack of background as a teacher and my unfamiliarity with the scholarship in our field made it difficult to understand how our readings fit together. But I remember the building in which the course was taught–Baker Hall, a brick and stone building that reflected the hedged bet Andrew Carnegie made when he founded Carnegie Tech, follows the slope of the hill along Schenley Park, which would have allowed Carnegie to repurpose the building as an assembly line had the fledgling institution failed. And I remember our seminar room, with a large square table surrounded by chairs holding a dozen students, a set of mismatched posters on its walls, and a bank of windows overlooking the quad one floor below. And, most vividly, I remember the way Mike taught. It's something I remember whenever I plan a class; I can't recall planning a class without reflecting, at one point or another, on his approach to teaching. When I teach best (or, at least, when I think I've taught well), I almost always find myself reflecting on how close I've come to the example he set.

Mike's (Unintended) Lessons on Teaching

Mike's seminar was titled "Literacy, Cognition, and the Teaching of Writing." His syllabus opened with the following description:

> Our research and our teaching are built on assumptions about literacy and cognition, and the purpose of this seminar is to consider, from multiple perspectives, some of the assumptions that currently seem most prevalent in our professional literature.

Mike's course wasn't about teaching. He certainly didn't set it up as some sort of master class that could shape his students' pedagogy. But it had a profound effect on me, and the lessons I learned during my first semester as a graduate student have shaped a career that has now spanned more than three decades.

The first thing I learned from Mike was how to approach a course. Mike was true to his values. He rejected the concept of deficit learning and the medical analogies that so often accompany it, and he made his values clear through the readings he chose and the way in which he framed issues during class. As Kristy Lyles Crawley observes in her article in this special issue, Mike didn't view students' needs as a source of deficiency, but rather as "a foundation for building a network of support through accessible resources, peers, tutors, educators, and college services." While I don't have examples of other classes he taught to compare with my experience, I saw a strong emphasis on inclusion, unfailing respect for students as individuals with varied backgrounds and needs, and a welcoming attitude that repeatedly fostered thorough exchanges of ideas.

The second lesson I took from Mike's seminar was the care needed to plan an effective course. He was deeply committed to dialogue, both in the classroom and in his selection of course readings. In his syllabus, he explained that the course would be broken up into five sections—Current Issues, Historical Perspectives, Cognition and Literacy, Sociopolitics and

Literacy, and Developmental Perspectives—and that two related readings would set the stage for discussion of each section:

> I begin each section with a pair of articles, a couplet. Sometimes the reason for the pairing is pretty obvious, sometimes less so – but in either case, each article plays off the other. My hope is that the coupling will make a few sparks fly, not set a rigid agenda for the section following the pair, but generate stimulating issues that have direct bearing on the teaching and researching of writing in our time, and to which we'll return at various points in the course.

For the sociopolitics and literacy section, for example, we read Lynn Quitman Troyka's "Perspectives on Legacies and Literacy in the 1980s" and David Bartholomae's "Inventing the University."

Mike's course design provided me with three interrelated examples of effective teaching: the importance of developing a reading list that supports the creation of engaging activities and assignments, the important role played by thoughtful responses to student work, and the power of silence. We spent time during class writing in response to prompts he provided, and then either building on that work in a formal assignment or sharing our ideas during discussion. In my notes from the class, I found a passage that captures one of the important tensions that seems to have motivated his work as a scholar: "Key conflict: Researchers' penchant for problem finding vs practitioners' need for answers." While I don't recall the specific context of that discussion, I suspect it also reflects one of his teaching goals—and perhaps the working-class background we share: linking the work we do as researchers with the work we do as educators.

I've long tried to emulate the way Mike ran his seminar. I've often failed. But the goals were clear to me then and now: Set up the discussion; embrace the power of silence to avoid getting in the way of a good class discussion; and intervene productively but respectfully when appropriate. I have a clear image of Mike kicking back in his chair as a group of eager graduate students and faculty got into it. He used (his) silence as a powerful teaching tool. And it seems clear that this approach continued to shape his teaching. In his article in this special issue, Shane Wood quotes Mike's observation in the first episode of Pedagogue about the importance of listening: "I can't tell you what a fundamental pedagogical skill listening has become for me over the decades… I mean think of it, how many people do you know that really listen to you when you sit down to talk with them?"

Mike engaged in active learning long before it was an educational commonplace. Certainly, and I speak as someone who directed my university's teaching and learning center for eight years, active learning is far from a new idea. Our field, of course, has long relied on it. Yet the classroom metaphors we rely on—and this was particularly true in the 1980s—seldom center it. Before it was a hot "new" idea, however, Mike used it in much the same way that Chris Neuwirth used it in her hands-on, computer-supported classroom. As I look at his syllabus, it's quite evident that his use of active learning was an intentional act, not simply something he'd come up with on the spur of the moment. It was, effectively, an invitation to do more than listen and learn. It was an opportunity to start thinking like scholars, something he treated us as from the start. Seeing it in use in a standard classroom setting was eye-opening, and often challenging, especially when he asked us to write during class and share what we wrote. It's a practice I've used ever since.

The final lesson I took from what I now think of as Mike's master class on teaching was how to expand the classroom. His syllabus included a brief message about reaching him outside the classroom: "Office Hours. Plenty of them." Mike taught me by example the importance of being a human being rather than the embodiment of an institutional role. Because of my lack of experience in the field, I took advantage of his office hours. He was available and helpful. And while his temporary office was decorated sparely, it appeared to me as a warm and welcoming space. In our discussions, he helped me understand some of the issues I was facing as a novice scholar. He helped me begin to understand the profession. And he laid a foundation that has allowed me to continue to grapple with complex issues that have become central discussions in our field, including antiracism, classism, and critical language awareness, issues taken up by several of the authors in this issue.

What I took away from our conversations outside the classroom has shaped my thinking through a career than is now approaching its fourth decade. Mike's willingness to spend time with people is a theme running through this special issue. It proved particularly helpful for a new graduate student who was trying to make sense of a field he wasn't prepared to join.

Mike's work as a teacher set a standard that I've tried to meet ever since I took his course. His attention to detail, his preparation, his willingness to allow discussions to develop—and in particular his willingness to remain silent—have shaped my approach to course design. Similarly, his use of active learning and his availability to students have been deeply instructive. I would not teach in the way I do now had I not taken his class. I can imagine that the many other members of our field who took courses from him would offer similar testimony. His class set me on a path I've never regretted following.

A Closing Note

Nearly two decades after I'd taken Mike's seminar, I learned from a colleague at Bedford/St. Martins (which, disclaimer, publishes my textbooks) approached Mike about publishing a collection of his work. Mike seemed reluctant to do so, and they were willing to respect that decision. It seemed to me, however, that it would be a missed opportunity to share his work, some of which was available only through subscription-based journals, so I offered to get in touch with Mike about the collection. That renewed a connection and, really, a friendship that had lapsed as I had worked through the tenure and promotion process. After he agreed to work on the book, I was asked to review it. Shortly after receiving the review, Mike reached out to me:

> I wanted to take a moment to thank you for reviewing my new book with Bedford. I was reluctant to do it at first—couldn't see its relevance—but once I finally began, I got enthusiastic about it. Thanks for your kind words in reviewing it. Fortunately, I've got plenty of time to revise, so I'll be using your thoughtful suggestions. I am deeply grateful for your time and smarts. See you in San Francisco. (personal email, March 14, 2005)

My response was to thank him for doing it. I wish now that I'd thanked him more directly for everything I learned from him. His voice has been an important one not only in my professional and personal lives but also in those of so many others. It's a voice that reflects a sense of justice that goes beyond advocacy for any single group, one that focuses on the potential of each person. It's a voice that will continue to have an impact on the field, not only as an individual scholar but also as one working in harmony with the generations of scholars that preceded, worked with, and will follow him.

Works Cited

Bartholomae, David. "Inventing the University." *Journal of Basic Writing*, vol. 5, no. 1, 1986, pp. 4–23. *Crossref*, https://doi.org/10.37514/jbw-j.1986.5.1.02.

Rose, Mike. *Lives on the Boundary: The Struggles and Achievements of America's Underprepared*. Free Press, 1989.

—. "Rigid Rules, Inflexible Plans, and the Stifling of Language: A Cognitivist Analysis of Writer's Block." *College Composition and Communication*, vol. 31, no. 4, 1980, p. 389. *Crossref*, https://doi.org/10.2307/356589.

—. "The Language of Exclusion: Writing Instruction at the University." *College English*, vol. 47, no. 4, 1985, p. 341. *Crossref*, https://doi.org/10.2307/376957.

—. *The Mind at Work: Valuing the Intelligence of the American Worker*. Viking, 2004.

—. *Why School? Reclaiming Education for All of Us*. The New Press, 2009.

Troyka, Lynn Quitman. "Perspectives on Legacies and Literacy in the 1980s." *College Composition and Communication*, vol. 33, no. 3, 1982, p. 252. *Crossref*, https://doi.org/10.2307/357487.

Mike Palmquist is professor of English and University Distinguished Teaching Scholar at Colorado State University. Prior to returning to his role as a faculty member in the 2020-21 academic year, he served for fourteen years in various university leadership roles, including founding director of the Institute for Learning and Teaching (TILT), director of CSU Online (CSU's Division of Continuing Education), and associate provost for Instructional Innovation. His scholarly interests include writing across the curriculum, the effects of computer and network technologies on writing instruction, and new approaches to scholarly publishing.

Notes on Mike Rose

Lisa Moore

A farewell to Mike Rose on his unexpected death, this personal remembrance recounts Rose's generous guidance on the discipline for a new Comp/Rhet editor and his very human capacity for empathy and insight expressed by his devotion to the value of every person whatever their circumstances and the craft of writing.

I first met Mike Rose when I visited Elaine Maimon at Arizona State University-West, where she was Provost at the time, to introduce myself to her and discuss her book. Mike was speaking there at Elaine's invitation, and this, my first trip as a new editor for McGraw Hill, coincided with his lecture. I needed guidance on the various camps and personalities in writing studies, what the various approaches stood for, how they had emerged, who represented what approach, and who was leading the way in what a friend described as the Balkan discipline of rhetoric and composition (meaning, a dizzying array of diverse factions)—and whether he realized it or not Mike became one of my teachers. Elaine, Mort (Elaine's immediately engaging husband), Mike, and I all went out to dinner that night, and I got my first thrilling lesson on the democratic ideals of the discipline. I immediately read Mike's *Lives on the Boundary* and was hooked on what the discipline could stand for at its best. It was Mike, a textbook writer as well as a trade author himself, who told me to "get Duane Roen to write a book" and got a message to Duane that I wanted to talk to him about a book. Duane was kind enough to see me when I called (though it would take me several years to get Duane to agree to write the book, and only with the help of his future coauthors, Barry Maid and Greg Glau). Mike continued to champion the thinkers he hoped would shape the discipline (to me, as well as to others). And while I'm so grateful to Mike for all he taught me about the discipline, especially for my continuing friendship with Duane Roen, it was Mike's little idiosyncrasies that touched me most as I relied on his advice on various aspects of pedagogy or people.

When he discovered my daughter was having trouble learning to read in special education courses in elementary school, he immediately called a friend of his who lived near us and got a recommendation for a brilliant tutor to help her. He just couldn't abide the idea that any student would be written off the way my daughter had been. (My daughter is now in graduate school at Adelphi University for educational technology, after getting her degree—with honors—from SUNY Purchase. Thank you, Mike.) Mike continued to the end to ask after her and beam with pride over her accomplishments. He was like that, I believe, with everyone. No one was unimportant. As others have remarked in various tributes that I read after his passing, he made everyone feel like their struggles and accomplishments were as important as anyone who was famous or powerful (no small thing in the middle of Santa Monica's Hollywood culture). I remember him telling me once of a graduate student who had come in for orals and had brought a lasagna or some other kind of casserole for the occasion. The faculty who were there weren't especially pleased with her thesis and were guiltily avoiding the gift of food she had brought, so Mike—to make her feel more welcome and appreciated—ate so much of it that he came home sick from overeating. He always believed in treating everyone with compassion, dignity, and respect.

When I had my own feelings of inadequacy, he would remind me, "You are Jack Moore's daughter!"—knowing I had come from a towering figure of a father in a ranching family in Texas. It would always buck me up. He also had an abiding faith that work was redemptive. And in those moments where he reminded me of my roots, he would also tell me just to work at whatever I was concerned about and that work in itself would alleviate my anxiety. He believed, he told me, it was the engagement with work that gave life meaning and dignity. He himself was an example of that. Religious about writing, he often described it as painful and a misery, but he carved out a routine that gave him hours each day to focus on whatever work he was writing at the time. Nothing was to interfere with that precious time, not the phone, not email, not anything. No surprise, I guess, from a man who wrote extensively on the subject of writer's block. He was a painstaking writer, laboring over each sentence until it was perfect. I sometimes felt he even edited himself as he spoke; he had a deliberate and certainly thoughtful delivery. It wasn't a one-way street. I was happy to have been one of his readers on *The Mind at Work* when he was working on that book. And later, I was impressed that he managed to create a social media presence with his blog, given how little he really cared for the interruption of social media.

He also had a silly sense of humor, relishing in those little Christmas Santas that danced to Christmas music, and loved Day of the Dead paraphernalia, amassing quite a collection. He would delight in the first bloom of a plant he had on his balcony, and he liked to say "life is good" as he stood on Venice Beach where he lived for so long before his move to Santa Monica. To the end, what a humane voice he continued to be through his work but also through his little "d" democratic interactions. Just three weeks before he died, he had sent me his latest piece: an essay on how science fiction had helped him survive a devastating childhood. He wanted me to share it with my husband, whose early career as an aspiring fantasy novelist had become overshadowed by the death of his sister.

And then, the news.

In big ways and small, Mike's legacy lives on not only in his own work, not only in the work he's influenced in others, not only in the careers he's nourished and promoted, but as a testimony to the spiritual significance in the everyday and how much that example can usefully guide us all to make a difference.

Lisa Moore has had an extensive career in higher education publishing, publishing numerous award-winning and best-selling text and technology projects. A co-founder of a publishing services consultancy *Glen Hollow, Ink.*, Moore has worked with numerous scholars on topics as varied as gender and communication, immigration, child trafficking in Africa, AIDS in the global South, medieval history, and, most recently, the politics of water. She divides her time between Brooklyn and a lovingly restored historic inn, Glen Hollow, in the Finger Lakes region of Upstate New York. Glen Hollow is an official partner to the Academy of American Poets, providing residencies to the winners of the Lenore Marshall Prize.

Mike Rose and the University of the People

Shirin Vossoughi and Manuel Espinoza

This reprinted blog offers a dialogue framed as "a siblings' tribute to a giant" between Rose's students.

Shirin: Thank you dear brother for having this conversation with me. When we were in grad school together at UCLA—you a few years ahead of me—you taught me that our real home is the university of the people. That felt grounding. Like the real university is the one that's conjured when people engage in social dreaming and intellectual struggle toward the good, change-making work of the world. And: remember who you really work for. It's an ethic I try to share with my students. I feel like Mike was an architect and caretaker of the university of the people. How do you think that came to be?

Manuel: Sis, I only know—or, think I know—an aspect of this. It's like saying I know the sun when it falls differently upon each of us. Mike was loved. He also felt things like sorrow acutely. And, he had a gregarious and curious spirit. He was an artist, which meant that he liked to re-arrange things. What better to re-arrange than his life as best he could? All of this (and so much more I don't know) came together to create the conditions for a poor child to become a loving man. His cause was that of the person half-heard and nearly-discarded.

Shirin: You and I and so many others across time and place are the inheritors of that love. A few years ago I had a conversation with Mike where I mentioned the learning humanities—a term I first heard from you. I said it in passing, but he stopped me and said, "Wait say that again." He threw in some swear words as Mike often did. And then, "That's what we've been up to!" I think a lot about how he modeled the humanistic and artful design and study of learning, in his research, writing, teaching and being. How do you see his work in relation to the idea of the learning humanities?

Manuel: I see it as an exemplar, sis. It is a way of trying to be truthful in this world, a way of creating beauty. For we not only have need of taking in, drinking in what is beautiful, we have an impulse to flood the world with beauty of our own manufacture. The learning humanities is a branch of the art and craft of writing, one that helps us create portraits of becoming, which can be instructive and transcendent when labored over, when finely and attentively rendered.

Mike thought so highly of you, sis. What aspects of our dear mentor do you remember most vividly?

Shirin: The ways he moved through the world as a teacher stood so powerfully against and beyond systems of dehumanized learning. And, the ways he observed brought forward possibility. I remember the feeling of working to articulate a baby-idea in his presence at that round wooden table in his office, or sitting across from him in the red-lit Galley. He would close his eyes and nod as you spoke, taking it all in so he could get to the essence of what you were reaching for. He'd reflect it back like you were a bonafide writer and he was your most avid reader, and help you whittle and stretch and refine and sharpen until it sang. Then he'd call a few days later to tell you he was still thinking about a sentence or phrase from your piece. What a thing to hear as a young writer. I witnessed him do this many times, with my peers, and eventually with my own students when he'd graciously accept invitations to visit my classes.

And I remember the feeling of his handwritten No. 2 pencil feedback on our papers, a potent blend of no-bullshit affirmation for what was working and careful models for what could work better, and why. I often find myself channeling these ways of being with my students, reading their essays with keen interest, working to fade the boundaries between writing for school and writing for life. That kind of pedagogical care sows a loving responsibility for ongoing creation.

What do you remember most vividly brother?

Manuel: What I remember most was his loving kindness. A few years ago, a terrible thing happened to me. He picked me up off the mat, dusted me off, and walked alongside me, his hand on my shoulder as I regained my balance and came back among the living. His support, his encouragement, nursed me back to health, back to integrity. He was masterful at helping me learn how to become a sharper thinker, a more effective and elegant writer, a scholar with a flexible and fruitful process. The intellectual apprenticeship with Mike was life-altering, but what he taught me about being a human being, about being a man, held even greater significance. (To be certain, there were times when all of those things came together.) I was his student, his colleague, and, later on, his son. Engrafted—as another mentor of ours would say—made part of the living original by choice, with fatherly intent.

NOTE

Reprinted with permission from *Blue Dandelion: Sketches in the Poetics of Learning* located at https://www.bluedandelion.org/blog

Manuel Luis Espinoza is associate professor at the University of Colorado at Denver in the School of Education and Human Development, where he works on issues of learning and civil rights. He is a child of desegregation (*Keyes v. Denver School District No. 1*, 1973) and a Chicano ethnographer and philosopher of education working in the scholarly tradition that emerged during the twentieth-century struggle against racism in the United States.

Shirin Vossoughi is associate professor at Northwestern University's School of Education and Social Policy, where she draws on ethnographic methods to study the social, historical, and political dimensions of learning and educational equity. As an Iranian immigrant and the daughter of political exiles, she is invested in the development of educational settings for youth from migrant, immigrant, and diasporic backgrounds.

The Small Stuff

John Alberti

Drawing on the author's experience as a graduate student in Mike Rose's practicum on teaching, the essay discusses the foundational importance of "small things," as Rose called them. The author describes how Rose's teaching provided him an opportunity to experience the "micro-evidence of care" in Rose's classroom interactions and the profound effect that such a "small thing" had on the author's formation as a teacher and scholar. In particular, the essay stresses the essential importance of focusing on the unique singularity of each student writer to inform how we think about teaching and how we think about the mission and purpose of writing programs.

> *I value the small stuff. The teacher who encourages a hesitant question; who remembers a student's name outside the classroom; who in discussing a paper suggests a book, a podcast, a movie; who spends an extra five minutes in a conference; who checks in with a student who had difficulty with the last assignment. These are everyday signs of commitment, micro-evidence of care (Mike Rose, "The Everyday Gestures of Justice").*

Fall term, 1982. It was the first day of our graduate practicum in how to teach a writing class (the course had a more official-sounding title, but that's really what it was). I was in my second year of graduate school in English, having come to UCLA after a first year at Cal Berkeley the year before that had led me to quit grad school altogether. No knock on Berkeley; I had some great teachers there, and the bay area is fantastic. I was just fed up with eighteen years of tests and grades, of constantly being evaluated to see if I remained worthy of further education. I had only come to graduate school in the first place because of a suggestion by my undergraduate Shakespeare professor. It was a real act of encouragement and kindness (see epigraph above), and although I knew nothing about graduate school, or where it might lead, I liked learning and I didn't have any other plans for what I might do next, so off to Berkeley I went.

A sobering encounter with corporate job prospects over the summer changed my mind about grad school, and so back I went, this time closer to home at UCLA. There I was offered the chance to become a teaching assistant leading my own composition course, a prospect I found both intriguing and terrifying. Like everyone, I had my own long history with all sorts of teachers and teaching strategies, and I knew what I liked and what I didn't. Still, I didn't have any systematic beliefs about pedagogy. A chance encounter with *Zen and the Art of Motorcycle Maintenance* in an undergrad writing class had blown my mind a bit with its iconoclastic takes on formal education—especially the argument that grades deter learning and promote conformity—but when I walked into that practicum, I was looking for a plan and guidebook, or at the very least a survival strategy.

I discovered many things that first term: that there was a whole field of English studies called Composition and Rhetoric (who knew?), that there was a whole body of research and theorizing about what actually happens in our brains when we put pen to paper or fingers to keyboard, and that I was fascinated by it all. Mostly, though, I discovered Mike Rose, who was team teaching the practicum along with Carol Hartzog. At the time, Mike Rose was not yet "Mike Rose," a name instantly recognized in our field and representing a body of work that has become indispensable for any teacher, writing or otherwise. He was 37 years old at the time, just two years removed from completing his own PhD at UCLA, and still on the cusp of publishing the articles and books that would change how we think about writing.

But really, even at that early time, Mike was still Mike (would always be Mike). His relaxed, welcoming vibe (and vibe is the right word; after all, we were both California guys); his ready smile changing to a look of genuine curiosity for what *you* had to say; the way he made everyone in that room felt like we belonged there, that we belonged in a classroom, whether as students or teachers. Or rather, understanding that students *are* teachers, and vice versa.

Like any dutiful composition student, let me provide a concrete example. Before we dove into pedagogical theory, assignment design, or facilitating student peer review (still a radical concept in 1982), Mike passed around a sheet of paper with some writing on it. And what writing it was (I wish I still had that handout, but we often don't recognize life-changing experiences except in retrospect). As a sample of "standard prose," it was confusing. The syntax and grammar were unorthodox, the argument (if that's what it was) unclear or maybe nonexistent. I'm guessing I wasn't alone among my peers in wondering whether this wasn't some sort of trap or initiation ceremony, a "so you want to teach writing" gatekeeping exercise to see if we had what it takes. As Mike might say, those suspicions spoke to the ways years of formal education had taught us to always be wary, to always look for the hidden agenda behind every classroom challenge. As he also might say, those suspicions also spoke to how smart and savvy we were as well.

I still don't know what gave me the courage to offer my two cents: maybe it was a leap of faith; maybe a leap of "what the hell." Or maybe it was that Mike Rose vibe in the room (that's where I'd put my money). When Mike asked us for our observations about the writing, I offered that depending on how I looked at it, this could either be the product of a person struggling with writing or a provocative piece of avant garde prose. I couldn't say for sure without knowing more about the writer and what they were trying to do.

I still stand by this observation, even if it doesn't strike me now quite as profound as I hoped it was in 1982. But what has stayed most with me is the way Mike took my contribution seriously, using it to invite all of us to question the snap judgments we are liable to make about any piece of student writing and to always stay in the moment in our encounters with student writers. I know my observation wasn't a shocking new idea to Mike. But it did represent the spark of my engagement with the text, a curiosity on my part about the question at hand that had the potential to lead me and maybe the rest of the class beyond anxiety about getting the answer right, looking smart, or trying to impress the teacher (although believe me, all those concerns were there when I first raised my hand) and into the work and pleasure of discovery and creativity.

In thinking back about that moment (and I still think back about it often), I've come to recognize that what I had feared was the unoriginality of my comment was beside the point. It could be the kind of observation we all nod our heads at and say, "that's true, I guess it could be either unintentionally bad or intentionally provoking," and then dismiss to get back to the "real" work of figuring out how we as teachers should respond to the writing, perhaps with the goal of making sure it didn't happen again. But Mike led us to consider the full implications of my insight, if I can call it that. As we pulled on the threads of the idea that specificity and context are everything, that each writer and each act of writing is unique and ultimately irreducible to a type or specimen, so many of our assumptions about formal education and traditional pedagogies began to unravel. This was a possibility both fraught and, to a group of young grad students with years of a kind of co-dependent relationship with teacherly approval and validation, exciting as well!

And really, if all that happened that day was we left that first class excited about the teaching of writing, well, mission accomplished. But wait, isn't this story just another example of that co-dependent need for approval I just referred to? Perhaps, but all I can say is, this time was different. Mike's response was validating, no doubt, but it also felt genuine, more like a peer excited about my idea than a teacher bestowing his blessing.

In the same way, over the years I have read and learned from so many progressive theorists about writing and literacy, but when I read *Lives on the Boundary*, it was . . . different. Both intensely personal and deeply theorized, both layered with "micro-evidence" and presenting a historic panorama of literacy instruction in America, *Lives* showed me a different way to be an academic. It wasn't necessary to separate the personal from the professional; in fact, it was vital not to, despite the many messages to the contrary I had picked up as a student writer (and poignantly echoed in the question so many of my first-year writing students have asked me over the years, "Can I put my own ideas in my essay?"). His book exemplified how the work of the writing teacher is as much calling as it is profession, requiring both expertise and empathy, demanding that we bring our whole selves with us into the classroom.

So yes, Mike's validation and encouragement meant the world to me; really, in so many ways it helped give the world to me. The gentle yet insistent reminder that no work we do is more important than our engagement with the individual writers in our classes, that every piece of writing we encounter is a kind of miracle, and that every piece of writing and every writer contains multitudes, to paraphrase Walt Whitman; these values became foundational for me. Just as important, Mike made it clear that those writers included us. To Mike, we weren't just another group of new TAs ready to bear the load of teaching first year writing so the tenured faculty didn't have to. Each of us represented potentials that even we didn't realize, potentials to be good teachers, scholars, and even future WPAs, yes, but also to follow the example of Mike, to see our own radical potentials to change the world by providing the space for other writers to grow and flourish (not a bad vision statement for a writing program, by the way).

As Mike insists in the epigraph, changing the world involves the small as well as the large, the attention to each student in all their singularity and the absolute necessity that we keep that attention at the heart of the larger structures we build to foster that moment, whether in a course syllabus or a writing program curriculum. Call it the Zen of Mike. In my own career, I've used the confidence to try new things and challenge the status quo that I learned from Mike to work with others in creating large structural change, as when we rebuilt the writing program at my current university, and I served as the interim director for that program (and attended the WPA Summer Conference and Workshop at Purdue, another life-changing event).

That large scale work, the stuff that goes on a CV, is important, of course. But in the end, it's not any more important than the small stuff, those "everyday signs of commitment" that flow naturally when we approach each piece of student writing with a genuine curiosity about the uniqueness of that writing and writer, even after decades of teaching: expressing delight at a clever turn of phrase in a first-year essay; recognizing the bravery it takes for a student to question a long-held belief in a response to a class reading; letting another student know how their discussion board post made me challenge my own perspective about a film we were studying. The effects of these small things are impossible to assess in any systematic way, but as my own experience showed me, they matter as much as any carefully crafted assignment or course design. And if we lose our focus on the small things, the big things we make won't matter.

In the following years, even as Mike Rose became "Mike Rose," those small moments with him continued. I would occasionally run into Mike at conferences, for example, and no matter how long it had been since we last met, he would instantly recognize me, remember where I was teaching, and ask me how it was going. Another small thing, maybe, but also astonishing. It's a quality of concern and caring that you can't fake. I know scores of us have been inspired and motivated by Mike's writing, but those of us who knew Mike are especially lucky, because we experienced those ideas and beliefs in person, felt their power, and pledged ourselves to follow his example. Because of that small moment in Mike's class, a moment that was critical to my making it all the way to the PhD and to my career, I was emboldened to believe in myself and what I had to offer, to think both big and small, and to find a life I had scarcely imagined for myself before that day in 1982. As Mike taught us, that small stuff isn't small at all.

Acknowledgment

Thanks to my friend and colleague John Tassoni whose essay directed me to "The Everyday Gestures of Justice" quote.

Works Cited

Dettmar, Kevin. "The Teacher Who Changed How We Teach Writing." *The New Yorker*. 14 October, 2021. https://www.newyorker.com/culture/postscript/the-teacher-who-changed-how-we-teach-writing

Mike Rose, "The Everyday Gestures of Justice." *Mike Rose's Blog*. 11 April, 2018. http://mikerosebooks.blogspot.com/2018/04/the-everyday-gestures-of-justice.html.

John Alberti is chair of English at Northern Kentucky University, where he has taught since 1991. He has written two first year writing textbooks and several articles on writing in the digital age.

In Memory of Mike Rose

Ellen Cushman

This essay recognizes the enduring impact of Mike Rose on the field of writing and literacy studies, the quality of his mind, and his dedication to education, teaching, and learning.

Mike Rose knew no strangers. He was earnest, engaging, generous, and measured with his words. He encouraged, nudged, pushed, corrected, challenged, and questioned, and always with effortless charm and warm directness. Mike Rose was a scholar's scholar of teaching, learning, literacy, and education. At the core of his being, he held a bountiful vision of the democratic potential of public education and the everyday intelligence of students and workers. He held steady to the belief that the greatest potential of democracy was realized in a teacher's respectful challenge, a student's puzzling over a tough question, and a worker's clarity of purpose in efficient movements. He questioned the too-easy reduction, the minimization of complexity, and the simplistic platitudes that lend to impoverished portrayals of learners and workers, teachers and writing programs, poverty and immigration. His voice, deep and thoughtful, added to public conversations a steady measure of wisdom about the importance of education. Although his presence is and will be keenly missed, we have his enduring legacy of writing from which to draw courage, insight, and cautious hope.

Driven by his moral and ethical commitment to the issues that gnawed at him—injustice, bias, misrepresentation, or simplification—Mike doggedly pursued the everyday detail of intellectual work to represent the richness and difficulty of literacy learning, classroom interactions, and the intelligence of blue-collar and service work. He detailed the achievement and abilities of students, the painstaking work of teachers, and the lives and desires of immigrants. Mike lamented the slide of public discourse in America that too often placed the onus to change squarely on the shoulders of those least of all in the position to bear that onus. He would cuss with Italian gusto, then sharpen his pencil and write. Injustice angered him and fueled his writing. He corrected the public record, especially on the topics of school reform, student intelligence, the importance of writing programs, and the state of public education. He held the highest value for thoughtful and well-informed public discourse about blue-collar workers, teachers, writers, and learners most at risk of exclusion. He skillfully invited all of us to rethink learning in the context of abject poverty, overt and insidious racism, and lack of access to opportunity. He safeguarded these moral and ethical commitments in his research, opinion pieces, and blog postings. The strength we hear in his voice across these genres shall continue to inspire us as we endeavor to realize the most generous measure of democratic possibilities in education, teaching, and learning.

A prosaic aesthetic stirred Mike to represent the richness and complexity of learning, teaching, and working across the many genres of writing he took up. Mike loved a good turn of phrase. After a deep conversation with a teacher or student at a conference, he routinely pulled out a short pencil and pocket notebook from his well-worn jeans to jot a note about a phrase, who said it, and in what context. Sometimes he would read it aloud with an appreciative "humph," or a "that's nice isn't it?" or a "isn't that a hoot?" He leaned into conversations, especially over a beer, listened with a hand on his chin, deep eye contact, and earnest gut-core reactions—"huhn," "hmmm," or clicking his tongue as he carefully chose words for his gracious response. When he heard something that moved him, especially from colleagues at conferences who had waited in queues to meet him after a speech, he would lean in, close his eyes to focus on their words, and always have his fullest attention trained on the person in front of him. When conference attendees spoke of what moved them to learn, when and how they started, what they bring to the work they're doing and why, he listened hard. The details of every person's learning and teaching experience were equally worth his time and focused attention. The notes he took, the scholars he talked to and read, the opinion pieces and essays he enjoyed, and the people, above all the people, ignited the "craft pleasure" he took in his writing. Craft pleasure, "getting the sentences right, telling a good story" impelled Mike to render "experience in a way that readers can participate in imaginatively" ("Writing Our Way").

Mike strove to represent the challenge of learning. In the opening pages of *Lives on the Boundary*, Mike tells stories of learning, belonging, and mismatched expectations and skills. Bobby sat in an American Social History course Mike had helped to develop for underprepared students.

> He was watching the professor intently. His notebook was open in front of him. His pen was poised. But he wasn't writing. Nothing. I'd look back during the hour: still attentive but still no notes . . . So I sit under the jacarandas with Bobby. His girlfriend joins us. She is having a tough time, too. Both have been at UCLA for about three months now, and they are now in the fourth week of fall term. Bobby is talking animatedly about his linguistics course. It was all diagrams and mathematics and glottal stops. It was not what he expected

from a course about the study of language. "They're asking me to do things I don't know how to do. All the time. Sometimes I sit in the library and wonder if I'm gonna make it" (*Lives* 4).

Bobby wasn't alone. The jacarandas, glottal stops, poised pen, and blank notebook sheets of Bobby's story remind us how easy it is "to forget what a strange place" academe is (5).

His prosaic aesthetic fit hand in glove with his methodological rigor. He infused public discourse with the rich vocabulary needed to do justice to the intellectual intricacy of learning, teaching, and working. Ray Rosas's and Christina Saidy's essays in this issue make this point well. Stories were in the heart of Mike's research, especially his own stories of growing up as the son of working-class Italian Immigrants raised in soul-grinding poverty. The living memory of Tommy and Rosie Rose, Mike's parents, was everywhere present in his work. Many of his books are dedicated to his parents. Their lives and work stoked the tender embers of his storytelling, forming his earliest memories of precarity and dreams of a better life. Their lives inspired his own lifelong pursuit of literacy and learning development and his deep desire to portray the intelligence of workers, teachers, and learners. Rosie Rose waitressed. Interviews with her are at the heart of *The Mind at Work*. When she passed away, the words didn't come easily for Mike. "The sentences I formed in my head felt artificial, forced, as though whatever I wrote had to be weighty. If nothing else, it was awkward trying to keep the notebook open, standing in front of her grave, attempting to write something . . . lofty. Talking with Rosie could be funny, exasperating, heartrending, and you'd be taken with her wily gumption. But lofty? She'd think you were a bullshitter." From Rosie Rose's stories, his passion for dignifying the intellect of work took hold. From her skillful problem solving, he would hypothesize the myriad choices blue-collar workers make within the smallest of gestures. From Tommy and Rosie Rose, the sharing of their lives and later the memory of their lives, Mike would gather light, purpose, and an intensity of focus—the heart and mind of so much of his work.

The gross meanness and the paucity of nuance in public discourse about educating poor and working-class people really bothered him. His own teaching in low-income communities and research in schools at the boundaries of society's wealth demonstrated for him, time and again, the cognitive dimensions of teaching, learning, and working. And he used that understanding to counter simplistic abstractions that belittle poor people as underserving, or "sponging off the system," or a problem. Reductive descriptions of poor people and immigrants fail to accurately portray the living, breathing people that Mike taught and knew well. So he marshaled vignette, case study, and interview to describe literacy development learning and problem solving in loving detail with delicacy, spot-on accuracy, and unflinching honesty. Mike was sober about the significant challenges faced by people who are at the bottom of the income ladder. But he was, at the end of the day, also hopeful. Though Mike was "critical of standard practice and the social order" he reminds us in the introduction to *An Open Language*: "it is hope that drives [his] writing, hope that careful analysis and the right phrasing might in some small, small way open a space to think anew" (1). And that hope came from the very people of his writing.

Mike's methodological chops served him well to keep in check those outsized claims widespread in the media that diminish the lights of working poor, adult learners, young students, and teachers in underserved neighborhoods and community colleges. He gathered the concrete details of their day-to-day decisions to lend dimension to their lives, to show the complexity of the intellectual, social, and psychological terrains they navigated daily, to surface their values and hopes, and to make visible the hard choices and grinding challenges they faced just to make ends meet. He told stories to help policymakers, educators and future researchers better understand precisely for whom their work has implications. He understood that stories enact a social contract and animate civic life. And his stories were ever-so-close to the experiences, the lived realities, the messiness of intellectual work— there was no daylight between claims and evidence in his stories.

Learning and using methodologies for Mike served another purpose: methodologies are road maps into the intellectual workings of disciplines. As he grappled with a methodology, so too did he grapple with the restlessness and discomfort he had with professional confines. He opened up the inner workings of disciplines by studying their methods, and in doing so, he enabled himself and his students to achieve, to convey richer stories and understandings, and to have impact beyond disciplines themselves. Mike was sick of academic snobbery that demeaned applied work, especially the work of writing teachers, and that maintained rigid structures of access to knowledge, activity, and learning opportunities. "Intelligence doesn't reside inert in a discipline or kind of work or in one segment of a system rather than another; intelligence emerges in activity and in context" ("The College Cheating Scandal"). Mike was so dedicated to this unveiling the process of knowledge making and especially how it helped underprepared students and scholars to access disciplinary knowledge, he and Malcolm Kiniry co-edited a text and reader on the topic of academic strategies.

Mike loved teaching and learning and everything it revealed about students' intelligence. Mike Rose and Glynda Hull were among the first to challenge deficit-oriented assumptions about the linguistic and cognitive abilities of students, particularly for students labeled as "remedial," a programmatic label that codes for poor, black, brown, and/or immigrant students, and that masks in technocratic language systemic legacies of inequity and inequality. In reflecting on the Braddock Award Winning essay, "This Wooden Shack Place," which he and Glynda Hull co-authored, Mike explains that their intention was to "get in close to a moment of pedagogical interaction, to dwell on it in hopes of understanding its complexity and drawing something instructive from it" (*An Open Language* 239). This dwelling in and on pedagogical interactions between writing teachers and students points to another facet of the methodological rigor he and Glynda Hull practiced: it allowed the instructional discourse of teaching, learning, and writing to surprise, to spur the invention of meaning and knowledge. Dwelling in Robert's unconventional reading of the poem, "And Your Soul Shall Dance for Wakako Yamauchi" by Garrett Kaoru Hongo, they discovered a logic and coherence in his interpretation. They go on to propose an alternative to the template of participation patterns of classroom discourse (Initiation-Comment-Response). The transactive instructional method they propose places knowledge making at the center of classroom discourse: "the real stuff of belonging to an academic community is dynamic involvement in generating and questioning knowledge" (249). With Glynda Hull, Mike Rose helped to move the field of writing and writing program administration into asset-based pedagogies in 1990.

Mike had a great sense of humor, laughed deeply, and appreciated puns. The sonorous vibrato of his laughter could quiet a room. He could never remember the setup to a joke, but loved to repeat punch lines: "Wrecked him? Hell, it nearly killed him;" "Super calloused fragile mystic;" "Shirley, you jest." He appreciated the ironic, wry, and sarcastic comment, but remained wary of the sour nihilism born from the fruits of disinterested critique. "I suppose it is a good thing when even Ted Cruz is talking about economic inequality" ("A Reprise of Rags to Riches"). After he retired from teaching, he still researched and blogged and opined with that same hard-won balance of effective narrative and inviting prose. And he encouraged students, teachers, administrators, and scholars to do the same—to always think about our writing and research and leadership as connecting to issues of societal importance. He was compelled to critique, yes, but then to model and recommend and advise with emphasis on the cognitive foundations of writers, learners, teachers, and blue-collar workers. His wry comments were tempered with precision and the serious call to think and do better.

Mike Rose, circa 1991. Courtesy of Ellen Cushman, from Mike Rose.

For teachers of writing and writing program administrators, Mike's legacy of writing continues to inspire and be timely—there's something refreshing in returning to his work. And the essays in this special issue help to make clear why that's so. *Possible Lives* brings us into classrooms around the country, from the border city of Calexico, to Polaris and Missoula, Montana, to Tucson, Baltimore, and New York to see the democratic possibility of education. With his signature eye for detail, he revealed the professional perceptiveness of teachers like Stephanie Terry, Yvonne Divans Hutchinson, and Elena Castro who knew how to open up learning and language and science for their students and how to draw into their classrooms the people and communities where they taught. *Back to School* is especially inspiring for community college professors. Jensen and Hogue, Turner Ledgerwood, and Reid offer their insights into why this is so in this issue. *Why School? Reclaiming Education for All of Us* is a smartly powerful read for the bone-weary writing teacher and program administrator (see Newkirk, Moore, and Ritter's essays in this issue who also speak to the ways Mike's writing inspired them). To those new to research on writing, *An Open Language: Selected Writing on Literacy, Learning, and Opportunity*, offers important models for scholarship and public writing. The detailed ways in which evidence is brought to bear in those writings to make nuanced and impactful points are especially important. Mike's attention to details, gestures, observations, and explicit instruction, particularly as these lend themselves to interventions in public discourse, are remembered well in the appreciations offered by John Paul Tassoni, Margorie Stewart, and Ryan Skinnell, also in this issue.

Some days we may need to be reminded of the ways in which the work we do nourishes the deep systemic roots of democracy's possibilities and helps to redress its injustices. Mike's work will continue to nudge us away from the abyss of despair that yawns open just to the right or left of the good paths we're on as teachers of writing and administrators. And he knew this good path from the inside out, charting his own unconventional way from writing teacher to tenured full professor at UCLA. Eschewing his hard-won professional success, Mike always introduced himself as a teacher. He steadfastly honored the calling of teaching because teaching afforded him a dynamic way of knowing and being. Shane Wood makes this point beautifully in this special issue. Mike humanized the grand social contract of education in all he said, wrote, did, and spoke.

Mike championed the everyday intellect present in manual labor, teaching, and learning. He animated his portraits of teachers, learners, and workers with details that were painstakingly rendered through the eye of a scientist, the ear of a poet, and the heart of a humanist. He made everyone feel important and heard, even when he disagreed with them. Honest to Pete: Mike Rose was one the best. A kind man, a keen scholar, a model teacher, and a dear friend.

Works Cited

Rose, Mike. *An Open Language: Selected Writing on Literacy, Learning, and Opportunity*. Bedford St. Martins, 2006.
—. "A Reprise of *Rags to Riches, Republican Style*." *Mike Rose's Blog*, 8 Apr. 2015, mikerosebooks.blogspot.com/2015/04/.
—. "The College Cheating Scandal, Inequality in College Admissions, and the Preoccupation with Status in Higher Education." *Mike Rose's Blog*, 29 Apr. 2019, mikerosebooks.blogspot.com/2019/04/the-college-cheating-scandal-inequality_29.html?m=0.
—. *Possible Lives: The Promise of Public Education*. Penguin Books, 1995.
—. *Why School?: Reclaiming Education for All of Us*. The New Press, 2009.
—. *Back to School: Why Everyone Deserves a Second Chance at Education*. The New Press, 2012.
—. "Searching for Tommy and Rosie: What my mother's diaries told me about her life and my own." *The American Scholar*. March 3, 2022, theamericanscholar.org/searching-for-tommy-and-rosie/
—. "Writing Our Way into the Public Sphere." *Mike Rose's Blog*, 20 Jan. 2018, mikerosebooks.blogspot.com/search/label/Public%20scholarship?m=0.
Rose, Mike and Glynda Hull. "'This Wooden Shack Place': The Logic of an Unconventional Reading," in *An Open Language: Selected Writing on Literacy, Learning, and Opportunity*, edited by Mike Rose. Bedford St Martins, 2006, pp. 239-252.
Rose, Mike and Malcolm Kiniry. *Critical Strategies for Academic Thinking and Writing*. Bedford St. Martins, 1997.

Ellen Cushman is Dean's Professor of Civic Sustainability and professor of English at Northeastern University and a citizen of the Cherokee Nation. Her work explores how people use literacy and language to endure and create change.

Selected Works of Mike Rose

Kobena Bannerman-Jones

Books

Rose, Mike. *An Open Language: Selected Writing on Literacy, Learning, and Opportunity*. Bedford/St. Martin's, 2006.
—. *Back to School: Why Everyone Deserves a Second Chance at Education*. The New Press, 2015.
—. *Lives on the Boundary*. Free Press, 1989.
—. *Possible Lives: The Promise of Public Education in America*. Houghton Mifflin, 1995.
—. *The Mind at Work: Valuing the Intelligence of the American Worker*. Viking Adult, 2004.
—. *When a Writer Can't Write: Studies in Writer's Block and Other Composing-Process Problems*. Perspectives in Writing Research Series. The Guilford Press, 1985.
—. *Why School? Reclaiming Education for All of Us*. The New Press, 2009.
—. *Writer's Block: The Cognitive Dimension*. Southern Illinois UP, 2009.

Co-Authored Texts

Alkin, Marvin C., Christina A. Christie, and Mike Rose. "Communicating Evaluation." *SAGE Handbook of Evaluation*, edited by Ian F. Shaw, Jennifer C. Greene, and Melvin M. Mark SAGE Publications LTD, 2006, pp. 384–403, *SAGE Reference*, https://dx.doi.org/10.4135/9781848608078.
Christie, Christina A., and Mike Rose. "Learning About Evaluation Through Dialogue: Lessons From an Informal Discussion Group." *American Journal of Evaluation*, vol. 24, no. 2, 2003, pp. 235–43, https://doi.org/10.1177/109821400302400207.
—. "The Language of Evaluation Theory: Insights Gained from an Empirical Study of Evaluation Theory and Practice." *The Canadian Journal of Program Evaluation*, vol. 18, no. 2, 2003, pp. 33–45, www.evaluationcanada.ca/secure/18-2-033.pdf.
Cushman, Ellen, Christina Haas, and Mike Rose, editors. *Literacies: A Critical Sourcebook*. 2nd ed., Bedford/St. Martin's, 2020.
Espinoza, Manuel Luis, et al. "Matters of Participation: Notes on the Study of Dignity and Learning." *Mind, Culture, and Activity*, vol. 27, no. 1, July 2020, pp. 325–47, https://doi.org/10.1080/10749039.2020.1779304.
Hull, Glynda, and Mike Rose. "'This Wooden Shack Place': The Logic of an Unconventional Reading." *College Composition and Communication*, vol. 41, no. 3, 1990, pp. 287–98, *JSTOR*, https://doi.org/10.2307/357656.

—. "Rethinking Remediation: Toward a Social-Cognitive Understanding of Problematic Reading and Writing." *Written Communication*, vol. 6, no. 2, 1989, pp. 139–54, https://doi.org/10.1177/0741088389006002001.

Hull, Glynda, et al. "Remediation as Social Construct: Perspectives from an Analysis of Classroom Discourse." *College Composition and Communication*, vol. 42, no. 3, 1991, pp. 299–329, *JSTOR*, https://doi.org/10.2307/358073.

—. "Seeing the Promise of the Underprepared." *The Quarterly of the National Writing Project and the Center for the Study of Writing and Literacy*, vol. 13, no. 1, Winter 1991, pp. 6–13, www.hullresearchgroup.info/wp-content/uploads/2011/12/Seeing-the-Promise-of-the-Underprepared.pdf.

Katz, Michael B., and Mike Rose. *Public Education Under Siege*. Philadelphia: U of Pennsylvania P, 2013.

—. "Re-Imagining Education Reform: Introduction." *Dissent*, vol. 58, no. 2, Spring 2011, pp. 31–32, *EBSCOhost*, https://doi.org/10.1353/dss.2011.0039.

Kiniry, Malcolm, and Rose, Mike, editors. *Critical Strategies for Academic Thinking & Writing*. 2nd ed., St. Martin's Press, 1995.

Kintgen, Eugene R., et al., editors. *Perspectives on Literacy*. 1st ed., Southern Illinois University Press, 1988.

Rose, Mike, and John Martin Campbell. "One Room with a View." *Teacher Magazine*, vol. 8, no. 6, Mar. 1997, p. 32, *EBSCOhost*.

—. "The Prairie Years." *Education Week*, vol. 16, no. 25, Mar. 1997, p. 36, *EBSCOhost*.

Rose, Mike, and A. McClafferty. "A Call for the Teaching of Writing in Graduate Education." *Educational Researcher*, vol. 30, no. 2, 2001, pp. 27–33, https://doi.org/10.3102/0013189X030002027.

Rose, Mike, and Michael B. Katz. *Public Education Under Siege*. U of Pennsylvania P, 2013.

Public Intellectual Works

Rose, Mike. "2012 CCCC Exemplar Award Acceptance Speech." *College Composition and Communication*, vol. 64, no. 3, Feb. 2013, pp. 542–44, www.jstor.org/stable/43490770.

—. Rose, Mike. "A Language of Hope." *Teacher Magazine*, vol. 8, no. 2, Oct. 1996, p. 40, *EBSCOhost*.

—. "A Little School Under the Big Sky." *Teacher Magazine*, vol. 7, Sept. 1995, pp. 38–47. *EBSCOhost*.

—. "Blue-collar America is Smarter than You May Think." *Christian Science Monitor*, vol. 100, no. 202, 11 Sept. 2008, p. 9. *EBSCOhost*.

—. "Blue-Collar Brilliance: Questioning Assumptions about Intelligence, Work, and Social Class." *American Scholar*, vol. 78, no. 3, Summer 2009, pp. 43–49, *EBSCOhost*.

—. "Character Education is Not Enough to Help Poor Kids." *Christian Science Monitor*, 23 Jan. 2013, n.p. *EBSCOhost*.

—. "Chicago Hope: Comets in the Classroom." *The Nation*, vol. 261, no. 12, Oct. 1995, pp. 424–28, *EBSCOhost*.

—. "Community College: The Great Equalizer?" *Dissent*, vol. 68, no. 4, Fall 2021, pp. 63–70, *EBSCOhost*, https://doi.org/10.1353/dss.2021.0080.

—. "Double Shift." *Teacher Magazine*, vol. 16, no. 1, Aug. 2004, pp. 56–58. *EBSCOhost*.

—. "Education Standards Must Be Reclaimed for Democratic Ends." *Chronicle of Higher Education*, vol. 37, no. 42, 3 July 1991, p. A32, *EBSCOhost*.

—. "Giving Cognition a Bad Name." *Education Week*, vol. 32, no. 17, Jan. 2013, p. 32. *EBSCOhost*.

—. "Grand Visions and Possible Lives." *Education Week*, vol. 26, no. 7, Oct. 2006, pp. 32–33. *EBSCOhost*.

—. "Heal the Academic-Vocational Schism." *Chronicle of Higher Education*, vol. 59, no. 3, 14 Sept. 2012, p. 10. *EBSCOhost*.

—. "How Should We Think About Intelligence?" *Education Week*, vol. 24, no. 4, Sept. 2004, pp. 40–41. *EBSCOhost*.

—. "In Search of A Fresh Language of Schooling." *Education Week*, vol. 25, no. 2, Sept. 2005, pp. 42–43. *EBSCOhost*.

—. "Making Sparks Fly: How Occupational Education Can Lead to a Love of Learning for Its Own Sake." *American Scholar*, vol. 80, no. 3, Summer 2011, pp. 35–42, *EBSCOhost*.

—. "On Values, Work, and Opportunity." *Education Week*, vol. 19, no. 11, Nov. 1999, p. 60. *EBSCOhost*.

—. "One From the Heart." *Education Week*, vol. 29, no. 2, Sept. 2009, p. 27. *EBSCOhost*.

—. "Politics and Knowledge." *Education Week*, vol. 28, no. 16, Jan. 2009, p. 33. *EBSCOhost*.

—. "Reframing Career and Technical Education." *Education Week*, vol. 33, no. 30, May 2014, p. 33. *EBSCOhost*.

—. "School Reforms Fails the Test." *American Scholar*, vol. 84, no. 1, Winter 2015, pp. 18–30. *EBSCOhost*.

—. "Searching for Tommy and Rosie: What My Mother's Diaries Told Me About Her Life and My Own." *American Scholar*, vol. 91, no. 2, Spring 2022, pp. 80–93. *EBSCOhost*.

—. "Second-Chance Collegians: Inside the Remedial Classroom." *Dissent*, vol. 59, no. 4, Fall 2012, pp. 41–5. *EBSCOhost*, https://doi.org/10.1353/dss.2012.0086.

—. "Seek a 'Fuller Language of Schooling.'" *Education Week*, vol. 27, no. 11, Nov. 2007, https://www.edweek.org/policy-politics/opinion-seek-a-fuller-language-of-schooling/2007/1.

—. "Teaching Tools." *Teacher Magazine*, vol. 11, no. 7, Apr. 2000, pp. 40–44. *EBSCOhost*.

—. "The Inner Life of the Poor." *Dissent*, vol. 60, no. 3, Summer 2013, pp. 71–76, *EBSCOhost*, https://doi.org/10.1353/dss.2013.0060.

—. "The Mismeasure of Teaching and Learning: How Contemporary School Reform Fails the Test." *Dissent*, vol. 58, no. 2, Spring 2011, pp. 32–38, EBSCOhost, ttps://doi.org./10.1353/dss.2011.0042.

—. "Time to Help College Professors Be Better Teachers." *Christian Science Monitor*, 22 Mar. 2013, p. N.PAG, *EBSCOhost*.

—. "Untangling the Postsecondary Debate." *Education Week*, vol. 30, no. 34, June 2011, pp. 22–23, *EBSCOhost*.

—. "What Counts as Intelligence?" *Dissent*, vol. 61, no. 2, Spring 2014, pp. 34–37. *EBSCOhost*, https://doi.org/10.1353/dss.2014.0024.

—. "What We Talk about When We Talk about School." *Education Week*, vol. 16, no. 4, Sept. 1996, p. 38, *EBSCOhost*.

—. "When the Lights Goes On: How a Great Teacher Can Bring a Receptive Mind to Life." *American Scholar*, vol. 79, no. 2, Spring 2010, pp. 72–76, www.jstor.org/stable/41222187.

Scholarly Texts

Rose, Mike. "Reclaiming the Classroom." *Dialogue on Writing*. Edited by Geraldine DeLuca, et al. Routledge, 2001, pp. 9–29.

—. "I Just Wanna Be Average." *Lives on the Boundary: A Moving Account of the Struggles and Achievements of America's Educational Underclass.* Penguin, 1989, pp. 11–37.

—. "A Comment on 'On Literacy Anthologies and Adult Education: A Critical Perspective.'" *College English*, vol. 54, no. 1, Jan. 1992, pp. 81–83. https://doi.org/10.2307/377566.

—. "At Last: Words in Action: Rethinking Workplace Literacy." *Research in the Teaching of English*, vol. 38, no. 1, 2003, pp. 125–28, www.jstor.org/stable/40171609.

—. "Being Careful about Character." *Phi Delta Kappan*, October 2013, pp. 44–46. https://doi.org/10.1177/003172171309500210.

—. "Bottom Line: The Binary Ties that Bind." *About Campus*, vol. 13, no. 4, Sept. 2008, pp. 30–32. https://doi.org/10.1002/abc.263.

—. "Can Charter Schools Meet the Challenge?" *Education Digest*, vol. 65, no. 2, October 1999, pp. 50–55. www.proquest.com/openview/094c987c3c80726238b2d6bcb62e8749/1.pdf?pq-origsite=gscholar&cbl=25066.

—. "Devil or Deliverance? A Middle Ground for Grouping." *Education Digest*, vol. 58, no. 8, Apr. 1993, p. 55. *EBSCOhost*.

—. "Intelligence, Knowledge, and The Hand/Brain Divide." *Phi Delta Kappan*, vol. 89, no. 9, 2008, pp. 632–39. https://doi.org/10.1177/003172170808900905.

—. "Listening to Students: Coming Back to School: What Returning Students Can Teach Us About Learning and Development." *Change*, vol. 46, no. 2, 2014, pp. 58–61. https://doi.org/10.1080/00091383.2014.897193.

—. "Mike Rose Responds." *College English*, vol. 46, no. 3, Mar. 1984, pp. 304–06. https://doi.org/10.2307/377040.

—. "Narrowing the Mind and Page: Remedial Writers and Cognitive Reductionism." *College Composition and Communication*, vol. 39 , no. 3, Oct. 1988, pp. 267–302. https://doi.org/10.2307/357468.

—. "National Board for Professional Teaching Standards: Raising the Bar." *Education Digest*, vol. 64, no. 9, May 1999, pp. 24–29. www.proquest.com/openview/ba69269b8a15b097fa774f6231f5ed73/1.pdf?pq-origsite=gscholar&cbl=25066.

—. "Not Your Father's Shop Class: Bridging the Academic-Vocational Divide." *American Educator*, vol. 38, no. 3,Fall 2014, pp. 12–17, *ERIC*, eric.ed.gov/?id=EJ1044008.

—. "'Our Hands Will Know': The Development of Tactile Diagnostic Skill—Teaching, Learning, and Situated Cognition in a Physical Therapy Program." *Anthropology & Education Quarterly*, vol. 30, no. 2, June 1999, pp. 133–60. https://doi.org/10.1525/aeq.1999.30.2.133.

—. "Plugging in to the Global Classroom." *Education Digest*, vol. 58, no. 5, Jan. 1993, p. 36. *EBSCOhost*.

—. "Poor Kids in a Rich Kids' Curriculum." *Education Digest*, vol. 61, no. 6, Feb. 1996, p. 13. *EBSCOhost*.

—. "Questionnaire for Identifying Writer's Block (QIWB)." *ERIC Clearinghouse on Reading and Communication Skills*, 1981, pp. 1–8. *ERIC*, eric.ed.gov/?id=ED236652.

—. "Reform: To What End?" *Educational Leadership*, vol. 67, no. 7, April 2010, pp. 6–11. *ERIC*, eric.ed.gov/?id=EJ896440.

—. "Remedial Writing Courses: A Critique and a Proposal." *College English*, vol. 45, no. 2, Feb. 1983, pp. 109–28. https://doi.org/10.2307/377219.

—. "Re-mediating Remediation." *Open Words Access and English Studies*, vol. 4, no 1, Spring 2010, pp. 267–302. www.pearson.com/content/dam/one-dot-com/one-dot-com/ped-blogs/wp-content/pdfs/Rose-Open_Words-Spring_2010-3.pdf.

—. "Rethinking Remedial Education and the Academic-Vocational Divide." *Mind, Culture, and Activity*, vol. 19, no. 1, 2012, pp. 1–16. https://doi.org/10.1080/10749039.2011.632053.

—. "Rigid Rules, Inflexible Plans, and the Stifling of Language: A Cognitivist Analysis of Writer's Block." *College Composition and Communication*, vol. 31 , no. 4 1980, pp. 389–401. https://doi.org/10.2307/356589.

—. "Second Chances: The Value of Adult Education and the GED." *Phi Delta Kappan*, vol, 94, no. 6, Mar. 2013, pp. 45–49. https://doi.org/10.1177/003172171309400612.

—. "Speculations on Process Knowledge and the Textbook's Static Page." *College Composition and Communication*, vol. 43 , no. 2, May 1983, pp. 208–13. https://doi.org/10.2307/357408.

—. "Standards, Teaching, and Learning." *Phi Delta Kappan*, vol. 91, no. 4, 1. Jan. 2010, pp. 21–27. https://doi.org/10.1177/003172171009100405.

—. "Teaching Tolerance after Terrorism." *Education Digest*, vol. 67, no. 6, Feb. 2002, p. 4. *EBSCOhost*.

—. "The Cognitive Dimension of Writer's Block." *CCCC Studies in Writing and Rhetoric,* 1983, pp. 1–8. *ERIC,* eric.ed.gov/?id=ED230932.

—. "The Feel of a Writer's Work: An Inquiry into the Phenomenology of Work." *Vocational Guidance Quarterly,* vol. 29, no. 3, 1981, pp. 236–43. https://doi.org/10.1002/j.2164-585X.1981.tb01047.x.

—. "The Language of Exclusion: Language Instruction at the University," *College English,* vol. 47, no. 4, Apr. 1985, pp. 341–59.

—. "The Positive Purpose of Remediation: Getting to the Core of Higher Education." *About Campus,* vol. 14, no. 5, Nov. 2009, pp. 2–4. https://doi.org/10.1002/abc.301.

—. "The Stories Numbers Can't Tell." *Chronicle of Higher Education,* vol. 60, no. 35, 16 May 2014, p. B20. *EBSCOhost.*

—. "The Working Life of a Waitress." *Mind, Culture, and Activity,* vol. 8, no. 1, 2001, pp. 3–27. https://doi.org/10.1207/S15327884MCA0801_02.

—. "Tougher Discipline, Safer Schools." *Education Digest,* vol. 62, no. 2, Oct. 1996, p. 15. *EBSCOhost.*

—. "Vocational Education and the New World of Work." *The Hedgehog Review,* vol. 18, no. 1, Spring 2016, pp. 91–103. *Gale Academic OneFile,* link.gale.com/apps/doc/A448441359/AONE?u=nysl_ca_ind&sid=googleScholar&xid=2e7ca916.

—. "What College Can Mean to the Other America." *Chronicle of Higher Education,* vol. 58, no. 4, 16 Sept. 2011, p. A76. *EBSCOhost.*

—. "Why America Needs a Smithsonian of Basic Skills." *Chronicle of Higher Education,* vol. 56, no. 42, 13 Aug. 2010, p. A23, *EBSCOhost.*

—. "Writing for the Public." *College English,* vol. 72, no. 3, Jan. 2010, pp. 284–92. www.jstor.org/stable/25653029.

—. "Writing Our Way Into the Public Sphere." *Teachers College Record,* vol. 72, no. 3, 2018, pp. 1–18 https://doi.org/10.1177/016146811812001008.

Note

If we accessed an article from an electronic database and it lacked a DOI, we opted to eliminate the URL. Our editorial team believes that bibliographies should support rather than hinder the research process.

Kobena Bannerman-Jones earned his BA in English from California State University, Sacramento in 2019. He is currently completing his MA in Composition, Rhetoric and Professional Writing at the same university while working as a writing tutor for the University Writing Center and the Peer and Academic Resource Center. His future goals include pursuing a PhD in Literature and continuing his work in higher education.

Extending an invitation to join the

Council of

Writing Program Administrators

The Council of Writing Program Administrators offers a national network of scholarship and support for leaders of college and university writing programs.

Membership benefits include the following:

- A subscription to *WPA: Writing Program Administration*, a semi-annual refereed journal
- Unrestricted access to journal archives and job boards
- Participation on WPA committees and task forces
- Invitations to the annual WPA Summer Workshops and Conferences
- Invitations to submit papers for sessions that WPA sponsors at MLA and CCCC
- Participation in the WPA Research Grant Program, which distributes several awards, ranging from $1,000 to $2,000
- Invitation to the annual WPA breakfast at CCCC
- Information about the WPA Consultant-Evaluator Service

Membership Rates

- Lifetime Membership GOLD: print journal, conference registration, and membership for life: $3,000
- Lifetime Membership SILVER: print journal and membership for life: $1,500
- Member Level 3 (income over $100,000): $150/year (Green option: $125*)
- Member Level 2 (income $40,000-$100,000): $100/year (Green option: $80*)
- Member Level 1 (income under $40,000): $55/year (Green option: $45*)
- Student Member: $30/year (Green option: $20*)
- Emeritus Member: $30/year (Green option: $20*)
- Institutional Membership (1 print journal to institution and 1 WPA membership, including journal): $250

*Green option - receives digital journal in lieu of print journal

For More Information

Visit us online at http://wpacouncil.org.

PARLOR PRESS
EQUIPMENT FOR LIVING

New Series!

Studies in Rhetorics and Feminism
 Series Editors: Cheryl Glenn and Shirley Wilson Logan

Emerging Conversations in the Global Humanities
 Series Editor: Victor E. Taylor

The X-Series
 Series Editor: Jordan Frith

New Releases

Global Rhetorical Traditions, edited by Hui Wu and Tarez Samra Graban

Rhetorical Listening in Action: A Concept-Tacticc Approach by Krista Ratcliffe and Kyle Jensen

A Rhetoric of Becoming: USAmerican Women in Qatar by Nancy Small

Emotions and Affect in Writing Centers edited by Janine Morris and Kelly Concannon

MLA Mina Shaughnessy Prize and CCCC Best Book Award 2021!

Creole Composition: Academic Writing and Rhetoric in the Anglophone Caribbean, edited by Vivette Milson-Whyte, Raymond Oenbring, and Brianne Jaquette

Check Out Our New Website!

Discounts, blog, open access titles, instant downloads, and more.

www.parlorpress.com

WPA Discount: Use WPA20 at checkout to receive a 20% discount on all titles not on sale through September 15, 2022.

www.ingramcontent.com/pod-product-compliance
Lightning Source LLC
Chambersburg PA
CBHW031334160426
43196CB00007B/683